Kama Sutra Sex Guide for Couples 2021

You want to master the best sexual positions and discover new kinky ideas with your partner?

Copyright © 2021 All rights reserved

This document is geared towards providing exact and reliable information with regards to the topic and issue covered. The publication is sold with the idea that the publisher is not required to render accounting, officially permitted, or otherwise, qualified services. If advice is necessary, legal, or professional, a practiced individual in the profession should be ordered.

From a Declaration of Principles which was accepted and approved equally by a Committee of the American Bar Association and a Committee of Publishers and Associations.

In no way is it legal to reproduce, duplicate, or transmit any part of this document in either electronic means or in printed format. Recording of this publication is strictly prohibited and any storage of this document is not allowed unless with the written permission from the publisher. All rights reserved.

The information provided herein is stated to be truthful and consistent, in that liability, in terms of inattention or otherwise, by any usage or abuse of any policies, processes, or directions contained within is the solitary and utter responsibility of the recipient reader. Under no circumstances will any legal responsibility or blame be held against the publisher for any reparation, damages, or monetary loss due to the information herein, either directly or indirectly.

Respective authors own all copyrights not held by the publisher.

The information herein is offered for informational purposes solely and is universal as s0. The presentation of the information is without a contract or any type of guaranteed assurance.

The trademarks that are used are without any consent, and the publication of the trademark is without permission or backing by the trademark owner.
All trademarks and brands within this book are for clarifying purposes only and are owned by the owners themselves, not affiliated with this document.

Contents

Title Page
Copyright
Introduction
Chapter 1: Your First Steps into Kama Sutra
1.1 The Meaning
1.2 Purusharthas: The Four Main Goals of Life
1.3 History of Kama Sutra
Chapter 2: The First Stage of Lovemaking - Preparation
2.1 Seduction and respect
2.2 Leave The rest of the world outside
2.3 Setting the scene
2.4 Twelve Embraces
Chapter 3: The Second Stage of Lovemaking – Foreplay
3.1 Erogenous zones
3.2 The Different Types of Kiss
3.3 Scratching
3.4 Eight Bites of Love
3.5 Sucking the Mango Fruit: Fellatio Techniques
3.6 Let Your Senses Evolve
Chapter 4: The Third Stage of Lovemaking - Sexual Congress
4.1 Sex Positions
4.2 Improve missionary sex
4.3 Beyond the G-Spot
4.4 Sex positions to overcome anxiety and insecurity
Chapter 5: The Fourth Stage of Lovemaking – After Play
5.1 Pillow Talk
5.2 Kiss Each Other
5.3 A Romantic Shower
5.4 Cuddling together
5.5 Enjoy a chuckle
Chapter 6: Ideas to Improve Your Sex Life

6.1 Being vocal in the bedroom
6.2 Roleplay
6.3 Tease and denial
6.3 Bondage
6.4 Foot fetish
6.5 Spanking
6.6 Anal play & sex
6.7 Beyond the bedroom
6.8 Cuckolding
6.9 Food play
6.10 Sensory deprivation
6.11 Sex toys
6.12 Aphrodisiacs
6.13 Exercises to improve sexual performance
20 Minutes training
Try Yoga
Conclusion

Introduction

In Sanskrit, the Kama Sutra - or "love scripture" - is one of the most known texts on love and sexuality from ancient India. In this opera, we will explore some aspects covered in the original text and see how they are relevant to modern relationships.

This book is aimed at experienced couples and individuals who are going to begin a relationship. It is for the individuals who do not just want to stop at the sexual act, but they want to improve their relationship in every aspect. Furthermore, particularly for those for whom love and trust are equivalent words, who are prepared not exclusively to take yet, in addition, to give something as a tradeoff.

This book will help you build a stronger relationship, avoid the most common mistakes, and break down the obstacles that prevent you from achieving pleasure.

What is more, this isn't unexpected, because we are on the whole individuals of Western culture. In the interim, Eastern demeanor to erotic love is drastically not quite the same as the sexual culture of the West.

It might not come as a surprise, but the concept of sensuality in Eastern culture is vastly different from what can be found in Western cultures. In Hinduism, the body and otherworldly life, sexuality, and purity were viewed as a single entity. All the old-fashioned oriental compositions on the craft of love were committed to the mystical side of sex, and the Kama Sutra is maybe perhaps the most popular.

Even today, the Kama Sutra continues to help countless couples, assisting them with figuring out how to control their mind, body, feelings, and sexual arousal, permitting them to discover opportunity and congruity in personal life.

In this book, I will do my best to explain the core of the Kama Sutra and all its various facets. We will discuss areas like foreplay, flirting, sensual fantasies, fetishes, and everything that can be used to improve the relationship with your partner and keep the spark alive.

By perusing this book, you will locate a whole armory of all sexual positions introduced in the Kama Sutra.

You will become more familiar with magical sexual ceremonies, strategies for postponing orgasm, oral sex, and different parts of sexuality. I will do my best to pass on the information contained in the Kama Sutra, in a basic and clear language, in a structure wholly adjusted to the view of the individual of our day.

Bit by bit, this book inspects all the normal strides of sexual intercourse between partners - from the principal kisses and lovemaking to the mysteries of a fantastic orgasm. The variety of procedures and techniques contained in this book will not permit your relationship to transform into a daily schedule. The other way around, you can continually find an ever-increasing number of new vibes that have never been capable.

It will not be too difficult even to consider dominating these stunts, and the result will surpass every one of your assumptions.

Thus, if you need to uncover your sexual potential and become an eager, incredibly creative lover, at that point, this book is the thing that you need!

Chapter 1: Your First Steps into Kama Sutra

1.1 The Meaning

The Kama Sutra is an ancient Indian book that reviews human sexual conduct. It is viewed as vital work in Sanskrit writing, which has love, desire, happiness, energy, and sensuality, just as sexuality in the strict sense.

The Kama Sutra was composed around the second century by Vatsyayana, and the genuine title of the book is Vatsyayana Kama Sutra, or "Maxims on the love of Vatsyayana."

It is believed that some parts of the Kama Sutra have been added posthumously. For instance, the original text did not contain the different types of kisses. These techniques have been added by a translator who wished to make the book more useful for modern couples.

In addition to a varied range of sexual positions, the original text includes many other topics, among which we can find:

- Proper grooming and self-care
- Etiquette, including appropriate post-coital conversation
- The practice of the arts, ranging from poetry to cooking to mixing perfumes
- Discretion in conducting affairs, particularly adulterous ones
- Homosexual desire
- Female sexuality

The Kama is part of the four permissible goals of Hindu life and commonly refers to pleasure. In the following chapter, we will see each of these goals in more detail.

1.2 Purusharthas: The Four Main Goals of Life

According to ancient Indian philosophy, every human has four good goals, called Purushartha. They are the pillars that define a satisfying, meaningful life. Being able to live according to these ideals is not easy but highly satisfying.

Dharma: This is the desire to live righteously and do good deeds. For Hindu, *Dharma* includes moral rights, religious duties, and duties of each individual. It is essential to understand your ethical obligations and follow them; otherwise, you will have many regrets and end up in an unpleasant situation where you always look over your shoulder for karma coming to get you.

Artha: *Artha* has many meanings; it can be translated as "wealth," "money," "resources," or "means of life." But here, it refers specifically to material wealth or prosperity. It does not refer to the mindless accumulation of money; instead, it means working hard to achieve financial stability and economic prosperity.

Kama: the *Kama* signifies passions, emotions, desire for sensual pleasure. The *Kama* can be defined as "love without violating *Dharma*" (your moral responsibilities). It also includes worldly pleasures such as fine food and leisure activities like reading or watching movies.

Moksha: *Moksha* is the desire to let go of all worldly desires and find true enlightenment. In some interpretations connotes freedom from the cycle of death and rebirth, while others signify self-knowledge, self-realization, and liberation in this life. Some people are content to have these three first, but you should stand firm in your beliefs and make whatever sacrifices are necessary to achieve the fourth!

1.3 History of Kama Sutra

The Kama Sutra is an ancient Indian Sanskrit text on sensuality, the specific date that the Kama Sutra was composed is not known. Yet, gauges place it anyplace between 400 BCE and 300 CE. What we do know, notwithstanding, is that it was authoritatively accumulated and transformed into the book that we know today in the second century. However, this does not mean that the book has not gone through updates from that point forward. A few researchers accept that the adaptation we have is entirely connected to the third century, as a portion of the references all through would not have been relevant to the second century. With the content being so old, dating the manuscript is practically impossible. The opera is attributed to Vatsyayana, an ancient Indian philosopher that lived in India (Pataliputra) during the second CE.

Despite the common conception that it is a book containing mainly sexual positions, the Kama Sutra is much more than this. It is written as a guide to the art of living well, understanding the nature of love, finding a life partner, or keeping the flame of passion alight.

It is essential to realize that Kama Sutra never stops evolving. What was relevant a few centuries ago might be less important now, but the core principles of the Kama Sutra are always current.

After this brief introduction to Kama Sutra, we will dive directly into the middle of the action. According to the original text, the act of lovemaking is divided into four steps, all equally important:

- Preparation
- Foreplay
- Sexual Congress
- Afterplay

Each of these steps will be deepened in the course of this book and, if necessary, enriched with a more modern vision.

Chapter 2: The First Stage of Lovemaking - Preparation

2.1 Seduction and respect

Even if it does not include new exotic sexual positions, the preparation stage is crucial for the Kama Sutra. And in the original text, ample space is devoted to this topic.

An essential part of the Kama Sutra is dedicated to *the art of seduction* and its many facets. One of the main differences between the ancient world and the modern lies in the beliefs about the origin of passion. In the contemporary world, we tend to associate love with a partially mystical and partially biological force. Therefore, countless studies on the subject aim to motivate attraction with the production of certain substances in our bodies.

In ancient India, it was believed that passion was controllable by the individual, that it was possible to create and maintain sexual attraction through various erotic practices. The ancient Indians did not understand the chemical reactions in our bodies and believed that passion was a force subject to a well-trained mind.

The original version of the Kama Sutra was full of seduction advice. Some might sound strange nowadays, while others might be helpful if interpreted in a modern key.

Play hard to get

The original text advises women to push men away (at first), especially during the first dates; women should try to reduce physical contact and make themselves desired as much as possible. Yes, we all know this story. But, I think, a couple of thousand years ago, this advice might not have been so obvious!

The text also contains a strategy for men, which consists of frequently yawning and touching their mustache. Ok, this doesn't make much sense.

However, we must bear in mind that "*Play hard to get*," according to science, works. A study published in "Psychological sciences" entitled "*He loves me, He loves me not ...: uncertainty can increase romantic attraction*" proved the validity of the theory through a social experiment.

The researchers showed to several women Facebook profiles of possible partners. First, a group of women was told that the man found them extremely attractive and would like to have a first date. Then, the second group of women was told that the potential partner found them attractive enough, while the last group of women was told that the partner was unsure of his feelings towards them. Guess which men were found sexier by women? Primarily those belonging to the last group, men uncertain of their feelings!

Seduction is about the ritual

In the original version of the Kama Sutra, various courtship rituals were described, which today would no longer make much sense. Nothing was left to chance, and everything was carefully orchestrated to achieve the maximum chance of success. I do not think we would have anything to learn from these rituals if taken literally. At least, I do not see how it would help me in real life to tickle my partner's feet with lotus flowers. However, we can learn as a lesson to regularly allocate enough time to spend with the person we love. Create your ritual, choose a night of the week, and make it your special evening. <u>Despite all the problems and stress you may have, make room for one night a week and spend it with your partner!</u>

Respect your partner

I have to be honest with you; the Kama Sutra is full of patriarchal nonsense. However, we must never forget that the text was written in ancient times and from a completely different culture. Despite this, the Kama Sutra contains some pearls of wisdom.

For example, the book advises wives not to use harsh words with their husbands in public and deal with them privately. Furthermore, a wife should never divulge the secrets her husband confides to him. These, although obvious, are valuable pieces of advice that nowadays obviously apply to both genders.

It is vital to building a relationship based on trust and collaboration with your partner so you can create a protected space in which to be yourself.

2.2 Leave The rest of the world outside

Kama sutra is not for everyday sex; it requires time and patience.

Kama sutra can help to forget about day-to-day problems if both partners have the will to invest time and effort in achieving the pleasure together. It is essential to understand that Kama Sutra requires a particular effort, and it is crucial to allocate a reasonable amount of time to be spent with the partner. The end goal is not exclusively having sex but to get to know your partner intimately.

You want to build a strong relationship based on collaboration, trust, and mutual respect.

The first and more important rule is: **Leave the rest of the world outside**.

Decide for how much time you want to commit and make an effort to leave all the day's problems behind. Then, you must reach the awareness that for a few hours, it will be just you and your partner.

Leave all distractions, problems, chores, and appointments outside; it is just the two of you.

2.3 Setting the scene

A quiet evening at home might be just the ticket to a romantic interlude, or you might want to rent a room in a luxurious hotel.

Hundreds of ideas can help to set the right mood. Just keep in mind the relationship that you have built with your partner so far and what they like. In some cases, especially at the beginning of your relationship, you might want to keep it simple.

Here are some ideas that I hope can give you inspiration for your spicy evenings.

Get the right food: One of the best ways to enhance the mood is to make sure the room is stocked with the necessities. I personally love an excellent Champagne, but any other beverage that you both like will do the job. Strawberries or other fruit already sliced are always appreciated and can be used during the foreplay as well. Also, consider buying some chocolate and do not forget water and ice cubes. You may want to rehydrate during the evening or use the ice to play with hot and cold sensations!

Send your partner an invite and an outfit: You can surprise your partner by sending them a written invitation, along with a box that contains a fantastic outfit to wear. For example, you could pick something that your partner will like or think of your most favorite fantasy vixen and go with that. The right outfit could be the perfect opportunity to do some roleplay, realize your fantasies or simply be sure your partner is appropriately dressed for an elegant evening.

Candles dimmable lights: With a few minor additions, it is easy to transform your house into the perfect background for sensual adventures with your partner. You can set some candles on the dinner table, near the bed, or on the edge of the bathtub. Changing the lights is a powerful way to set the scene; shadows and lights are the perfect way to make more appealing the old bed and ignite passion.

Sounds: Music can help to create the right atmosphere. Pick something that you both like, or go for less invasive instrumental music. You might also consider non-music soundtracks like various sounds of nature: waves, birds, wind, etc. If your house is a bit noisy or you are not alone, you could use a white noise machine to block outside noise and cover bedroom noise.

Smell: Perfumes and scented powders are lovely (if you do not exceed with them). I love to burn some incense; sandalwood, ylang-ylang, and jasmine can stimulate sexual appetite and increase sexual attraction. If this is not your cup of tea, you could lightly scent your linens instead. Also, scented candles and air fresheners are a good alternative.

Take a bath together: Nothing is better than taking a bath together to release the tension. Sounds, smells, candles, and dimmable lights can be used in various combinations to wash away all the stress and awake your senses. It is an extraordinary chance to purify your day out and start new with your accomplice. In the Kama Sutra, it is expressed that the two accomplices ought to be newly purified after going into the pleasure room. This is to ensure that you are perfect and that your body is attractive to your accomplice.

2.4 Twelve Embraces

In the original book, various types of embraces are described. They can be used during all the stages of lovemaking, and there is one for every different situation.

Embracing can be an easy route to start some foreplay or just a way to show affection to your partner. For couples who are obscure to each other, embracing is an extraordinary method to eliminate the distance between them. However, a couple who knows about each other may move toward embracing with a drive.

Some of these hugs will seem obvious and not particularly creative, but I have chosen to report them in this book for completeness. We must keep in mind that the original text was written at a time when it was not easy to deal openly with any sexual subject matter. For this reason, even an obvious list of hugs was crucial educational material.

Touching embrace

According to the original Kama Sutra: "When a man under some pretext or other goes in front of or alongside a woman and touches her body with his own, it is called the touching embrace."

This embrace is an unexpected soft touch. It is a subtle display of affection, reminding your partner that you are still there and of what is to come. Soft unforeseen touches throughout the day will do wonders in preparing your partner for the night of love ahead.

Piercing embrace

In this embrace, the woman bends a bit to press her breasts against her man's body to tease him. This will ignite the flames of desire between them, which in turn makes the man reach for her breasts.

Rubbing embrace

A rubbing embrace is a public act that shows both love and desire. According to the Kama Sutra: "When two lovers are strolling together, either in the dark, or in a place of public resort, or a lonely place, and rub their bodies against each other, it is called a rubbing embrace."

Pressing embrace

"When on the occasion of walking together a lover presses the other's body forcibly against a wall or pillar, it is called a pressing embrace." This, more than a single embrace, is a variation of the other embraces. It is perfect during pre-sexual foreplay; it helps ignite passion and raise the temperature.

Twining of a creeper (Jataveshtotaka)

According to Kama Sutra: "When a woman, clinging to a man as a creeper twines around a tree, bends his head down to hers with the desire of kissing him and slightly makes the sound of sut sut, embraces him, and looks lovingly toward him, it is called an embrace like the twining of a creeper."

It might be challenging to know what the sound of "*sut sut*" sounds like; what is essential with this embrace is understanding that it would just occur in private. This embrace is a very personal one and is a display of physical affection given by the woman.

Climbing a tree (Vrikshadhirudhaka)

The woman embraces her lover by placing one hand around his shoulder, reaching for the back with the other, while placing one of her feet on his thighs. Then she set the other foot on her lover's foot, just as if she were about to climb a tree and all her moves express her desire to acquire a kiss from her sexual partner.

Milk and water embrace (Kshiraniraka)

This embrace can be interpreted as dry sex in modern terms. According to Kama Sutra:

"When a man and a woman are very much in love with each other, and, not thinking of any pain or hurt, embrace each other as if they were entering into each other's bodies either while the woman is sitting on the lap of the man, or in front of him, or on a bed, then it is called an embrace like a mixture of milk and water."

The Kshiraniraka embrace is close to having sex, but with the clothes on. It is used to express passion and has a vast erotic charge. There is only a thin barrier of cloth to stop the couple from having actual sex.

The mixture of sesamum seed with rice (Tila-Tandulaka)

During this embrace, you lie in bed, either scooping or being scooped by the other. That is close to what this kind of embrace is all about. Whether you lie down face to face with each other or facing your back to your partner, you both should be lying next to each other with your arms and legs entwining each other.

Embrace of the Jaghana

According to the Kama Sutra: "When a man presses the jaghana of a woman's body against his own and mounts upon her to practice scratching with the nail or finger, biting, striking or kissing, the hair of the woman being loose and flowing, it is called the embrace of the jaghana."

Jaghana is the area between the navel and the thighs. This embrace mixes pain and pleasure and can be an extremely sensual and erotic experience. We will see later in this book, in more detail, the arts of scratching and biting and how these can stimulate sexual arousal.

Embrace of the thighs

This is a very simple embrace that doesn't require a long description; it is when the lovers squeeze each other's thighs with theirs.

Embrace of the breasts

This is the kind of embrace that would occur later during foreplay. According to Kama Sutra, "When a man places his breast between the breasts of a woman and presses her with it, it is called the embrace of the breasts."

Embrace of the forehead

According to Kama Sutra: "When either of the lovers touches the mouth, the eyes, and the forehead of the other with his or her own, it is called the embrace of the forehead." This embrace is a very personal one, with the faces of the two lovers coming into contact. Nevertheless, it is a gentle gesture of affection and suitable for any stage of lovemaking.

Chapter 3: The Second Stage of Lovemaking – Foreplay

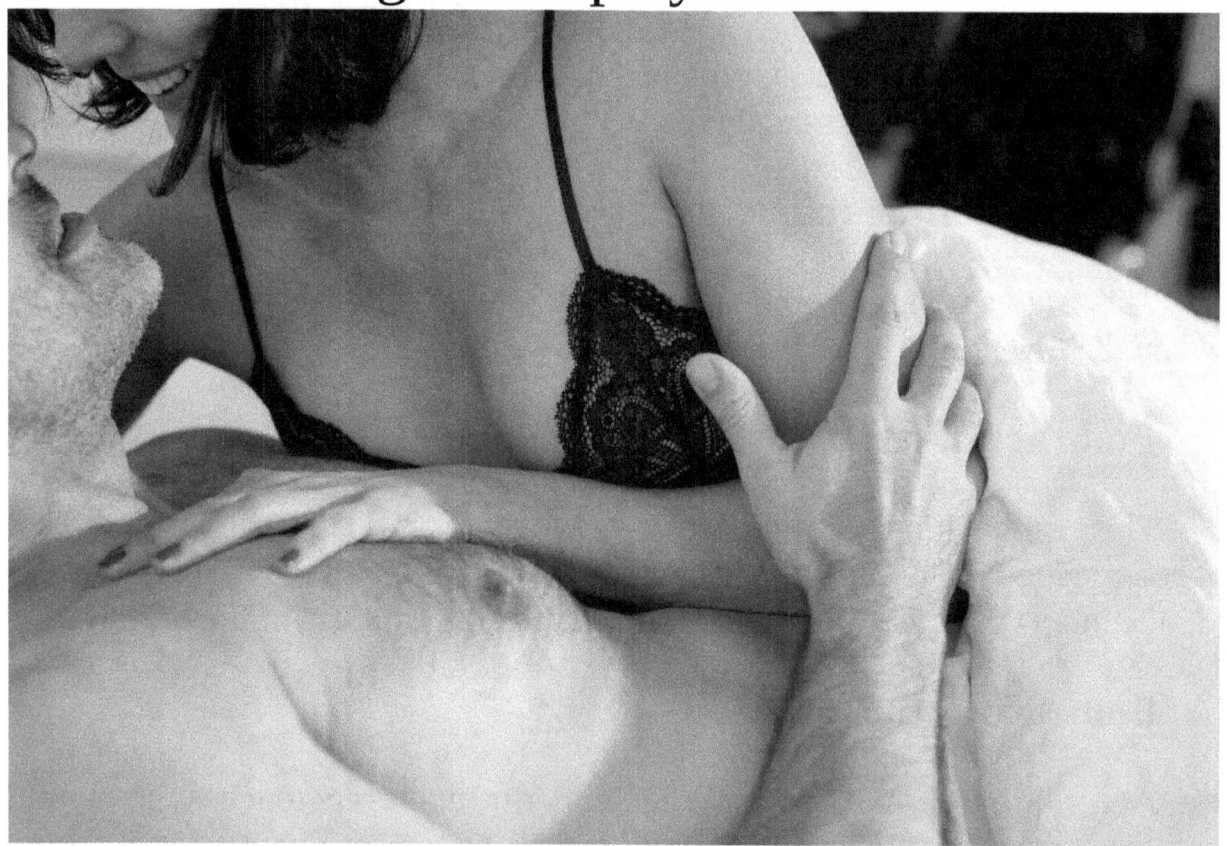

The foreplay is a set of emotionally and physically intimate acts between two or more people meant to create sexual arousal and desire for sexual activity. The foreplay is what warms the environment and leads to sex. Its primary purpose is to generate excitement and prepare the two partners to make love.

We are all captivated by the sex scenes of the films, by the garments that fly conspicuously all around, and by the bodies that rapidly end up between the sheets. In the collective imagination, this is cool and sometimes might happen, but in most cases, everything starts before, in a moderate and fragile way, without all the display. When foreplay was worked out in the original Kama Sutra, there was a reference to the servants who might help the man arrange the room before meeting with his lady. In the present society, large numbers of us do not have workers that we can depend on to do these things for us. Consequently, the content of this chapter has been adjusted from the way it was originally written. It is now more connected with modern society than to the Indian culture of a few centuries ago. This chapter will mix some techniques that were part of the original Kama Sutra with more modern approaches. Hopefully, you will find here some interesting ideas for your foreplay.

3.1 Erogenous zones

A wide range of areas can be stimulated from multiple angles during the foreplay to excite your partner.

Knowing where these areas are and approaching them is very important; this will ensure that both partners are ready and full of desire once the sexual congress starts.First and foremost, we will take a gander at the various zones of the body from which a person can encounter sexual pleasure.

Bottoms of feet

Feet have been the object of desire for a century. Some people love them, and some people hate them. Regardless of whether you are a foot lover or not, it is essential to know that feet have many nerve endings and pressure points; stimulating this often-neglected area with a massage or a soft touch can lead to pleasurable sensations.

Armpits

Inner arms and armpits are susceptible areas where many people are touchy. You can use a soft touch along this area to stimulate the nerves and ignite the flame. If you feel kinky, why do not play with a feather and torment your partner? Based on their body's response, you can mix tickling and sexual arousal.

Neck

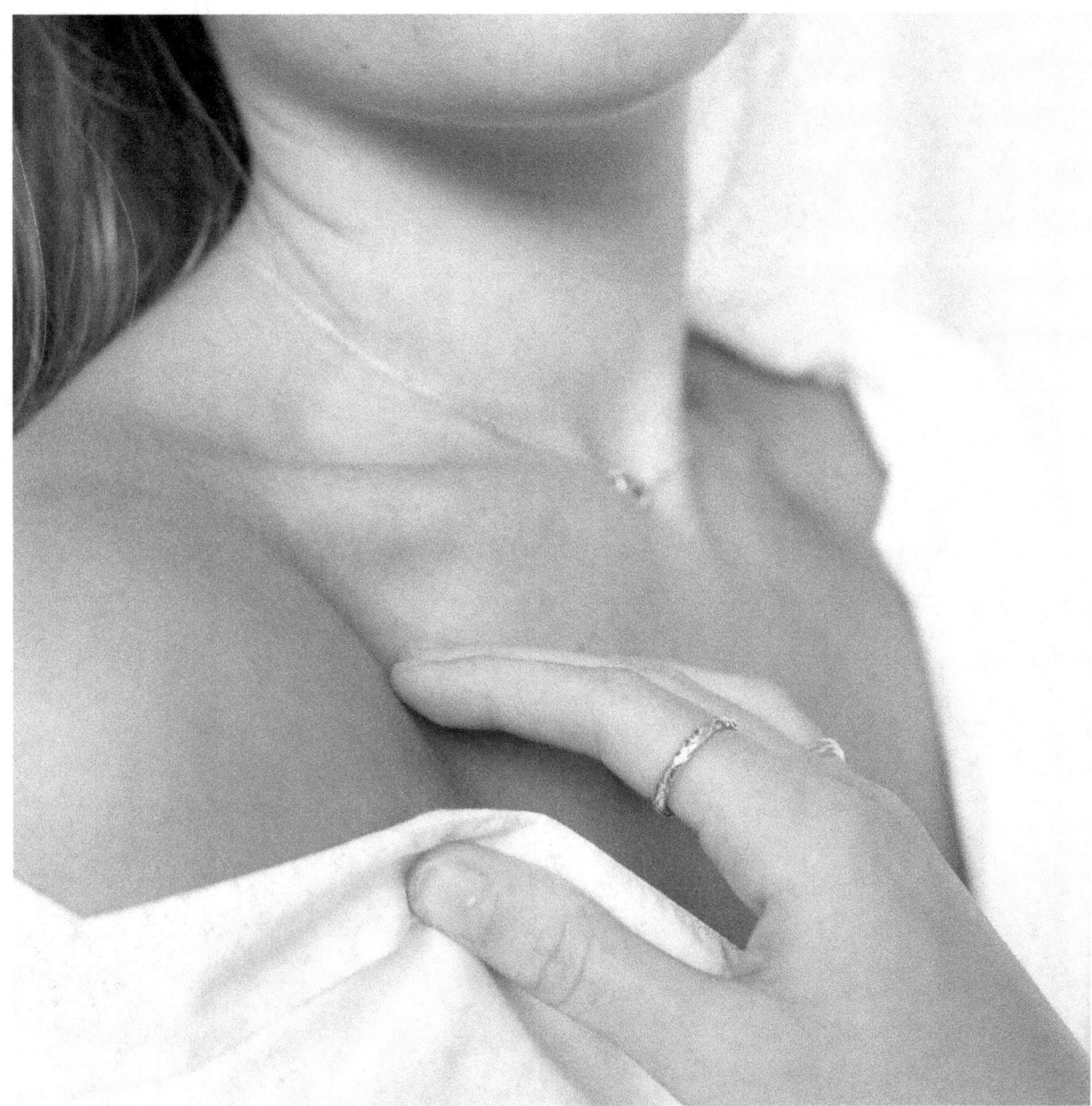

The neck is one of the most popular and sensitive erogenous zones, from the nape at the back of the neck to the sides below the jawline. Many people enjoy stimulation along the neck with a light touch or kissing.

Lower stomach and belly button

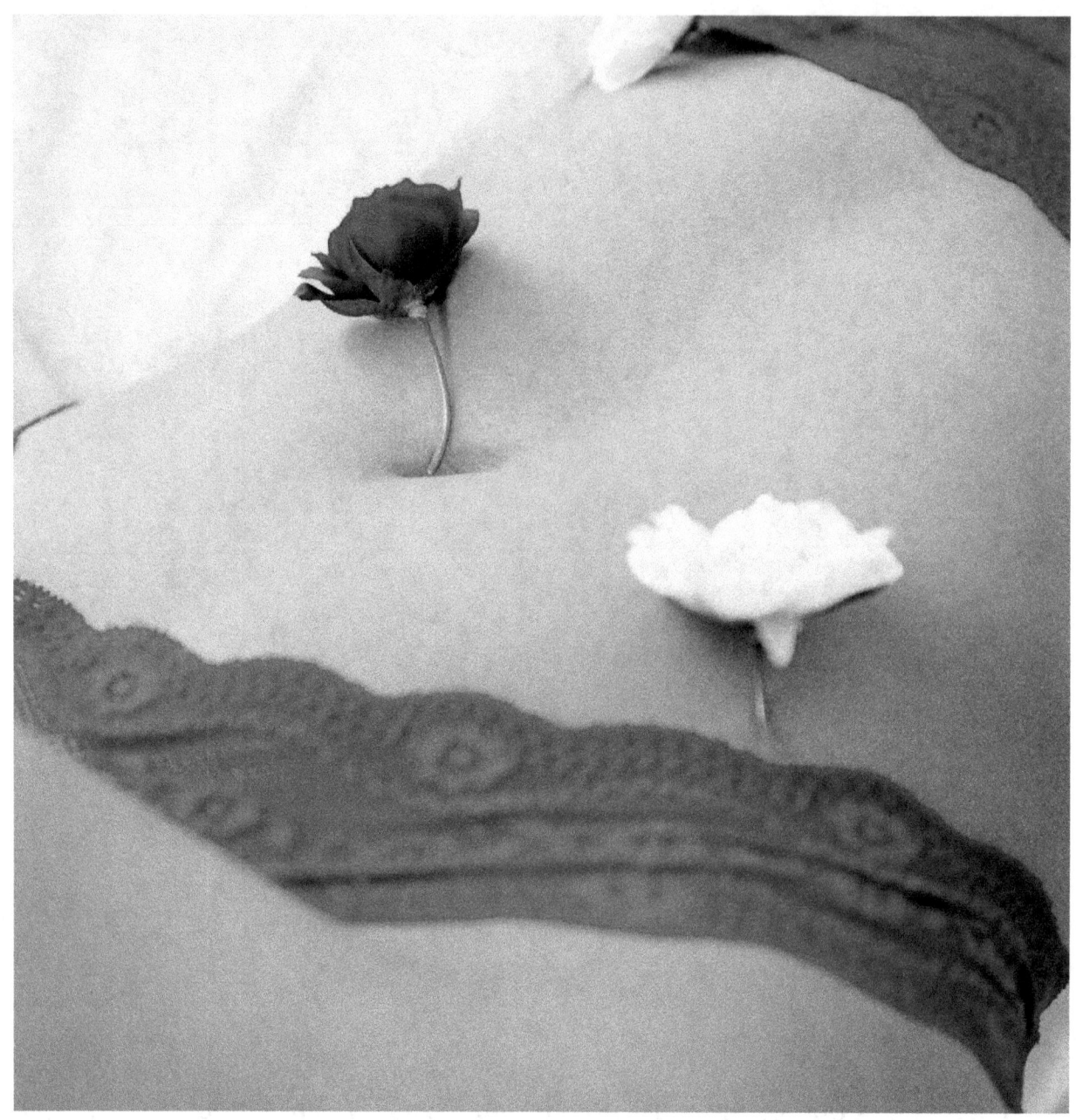

The lower abdomen and belly button are incredibly sensitive areas, and they have the advantage of being near the genital region. A light touch near these areas can easily lead to sexual arousal.

Behind the knee

This area might come as a surprise but behind the knee is another sensitive, nerve-rich area of the body. In most cases, this area is ignored, but trust me, paying particular attention to it during a full-body massage can elicit arousal.

Ears

The ears are full of nerves and sensory receptors, and they are one of the most sensitive erogenous zones in the human body. From the tip to the lob, there is not a single spot that will not elicit arousal.

You can play with them in various ways; light nibbles or kisses are a good ice breaker, and, depending on what your partner likes, you could bite even a bit harder or sucking them.

Hands

Hands, like feet, have many nerve endings that can be stimulated during foreplay. Fingertips and palms are particularly sensitive to licking and kissing. Slowly sucking a finger or kissing it can be incredibly sexy; also, as a bonus, the man's mind tends to associate sucking a finger with fellatio.

Inner thighs

The inner thighs are incredibly close to genital areas and particularly sensitive. You can try a light touch while moving towards the genitals; your partner will love it!

Genital region

Genitals are the most known erogenous zones and the ultimate source of sexual arousal.

For men, you can focus on the head (or glans) of the penis, the frenulum (the underside skin where the shaft and the head meet), the foreskin (for uncircumcised men), the scrotum, the perineum (the skin between the penis and anus), and the prostate (reached inside the rectum).

For women, you can focus on the pubic mound, the clitoris, the G-spot (two to three inches inside, on the front vaginal wall), the A-spot (four to five inches inside, on the front vagina wall), and the cervix.

Let's see in more detail the woman's genital region.

The labia are now and again alluded to as the "lips" of a lady's private parts.

We can split a lady's private parts into external labia, covering the internal labia, the clitoris, and the vagina. These areas contain many sensitive spots, which make them exceptionally touchy to contact and can, in this manner, give the lady colossal pleasure when stimulated correctly. The labia can be animated by a man's pelvic district or the base of his penis when he is penetrating her or giving her oral sex by utilizing his mouth and tongue. Fingers or hands can also stimulate them during foreplay or when the man uses his hands to invigorate the lady's privates.

The clitoris is the way to pleasure a lady. The clitoris is now and again alluded to as the female penis since, when a lady turns out to be sexually stirred, her clitoris will load up with blood and swell, making it increment in size like the penis of a male. At the point when this occurs, you can consider it a female erection. This means the extending or erection of the clitoris makes it considerably more delicate than it ordinarily would be, which prompts sensations of sexual excitement and pleasure when it is correctly stimulated. Doing this for quite a while in the correct manner can lead to orgasm.

The vagina is another touchy spot on a lady that can give her incredible sensations of pleasure when genuinely stimulated. The vagina is a trench situated between a lady's legs, prompting the lady's uterus inside her body. The dividers of the vagina contain a few places that, when stimulated, will prompt serious orgasms for the lady. You have likely known about the G-Spot previously.

The G-Spot is one of the spots inside the vagina that can give a lady orgasm. This spot can be stimulated with the man's penis during penetration or with fingers.

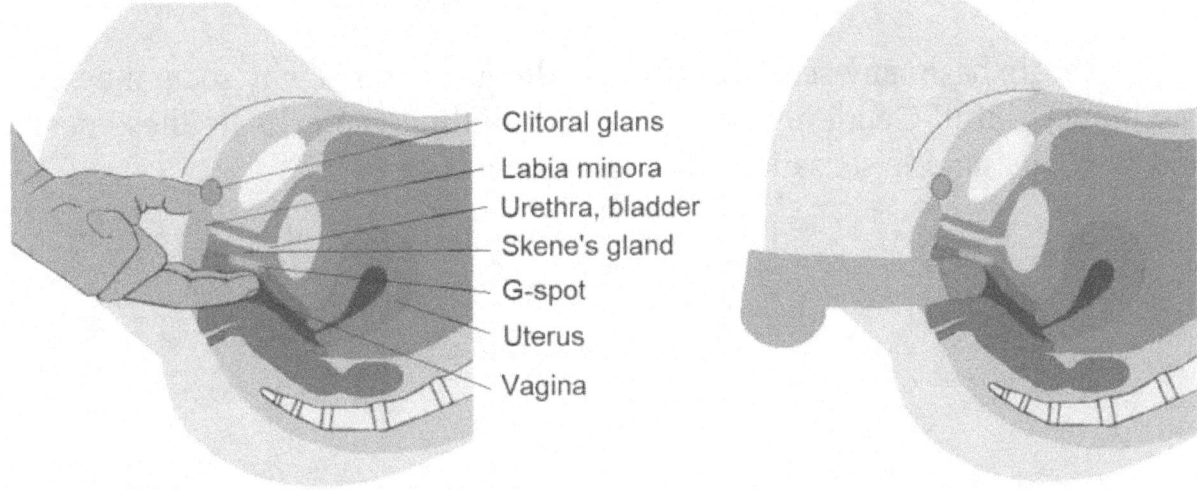

(Source: Pfaus, Quintana, Mac Cionnath, Parada: The whole versus the sum of some of the parts: toward resolving the apparent controversy of clitoral versus vaginal orgasms. In: Socioaffective Neuroscience & Psychology, 2016)

The bulbs of vestibule surrounding the vaginal orifice can't be shown in this sagittal section.

There are certain situations for the ideal points of penis-to-vagina that produce the G-Spot incitement, and we will take a gander at these later in this book. For the time being, note that the G-Spot will prompt an exceptionally extraordinary and amazingly pleasurable orgasm for the lady when stimulated. With the end goal for this to occur, however, the specific spot should be stimulated repeatedly as her pleasure builds right until it arrives at a peak, and she orgasms.

Nipples

The nipples and the areolas (or the skin around the nipples) are incredibly sensitive hotspots on the body and are closely tied to the sensations in the genitals. Many people vary widely in the sensitivity of their nipples—some are too sensitive to enjoy sensations, while others want rougher play, such as biting or nipple clamps. Each lady is diverse in how delicate her areolas are, yet numerous ladies can turn out to be sexually stirred by having their areolas stimulated. Nipples are an excellent spot to begin the foreplay; these parts are sensible and, with the proper stimulation, can turn on a woman in a few minutes. It has been accounted for that a few ladies are even ready to arrive at orgasm through areola incitement. On the off chance that your accomplice appreciates having her areolas invigorated, she might be one of those!

Scalp

The scalp has many sensitive nerve endings, which is why scalp massages can be delightful. Gentle massaging or hair pulling can activate these nerves and send pleasurable sensations throughout the body.

3.2 The Different Types of Kiss

In the original version of the Kama Sutra, there are described a series of kisses that can be used in various situations. Nowadays, some of them might seem obvious, but we must consider that centuries ago, there was no sex education or media to obtain this information.

Measured kiss

The measured kiss is when one partner offers their lips but does not move them. The other person touches their lips against theirs, kissing the mouth while the other stays passive. This kiss can still be passionate, especially if you are playing around with who is dominant.

Throbbing kiss

According to the Kama Sutra, the throbbing kiss is generally initiated by the ladies, and males are the receivers.

This kiss starts with bringing the lips close to your partner's mouth and gently press the lips against her lips. While the lady can touch her partner's lips with her hands or slowly with her tongue, her lower lip slowly moves to suck on his lips. At this point, the lower lip does the real action. This is a very passionate kiss, perfect for foreplay and sexual act.

Askew kiss

Askew kiss is perhaps the most widely recognized kiss for lovers to attempt. It happens when the two accomplices tilt their heads into one another as they press their mouths together. This position ensures that the noses do not disrupt the general flows while the tongues have the freedom to move inside the partner's mouth. This type of kiss is also called 'the crosswise,' and it is perfect for enthusiastic kisses.

Bent kiss

This kiss is also known as the 'turned kiss' and is probably one of the most romantic kisses in the Kama Sutra. The bent kiss is when one partner takes the chin of their lover and tilts it up towards them to kiss the lips. You can intensify this kiss by holding your partner's face. The Bent Kiss is ideal for foreplay as you are driving your accomplice towards more prominent sexual release.

Direct kiss

This kiss is also known as the 'equal kiss' as the two partners are on an equal playing field. The couple faces each other and kisses, licks, and sucks each other's lips. The tongue can be included in these kissing games. You can also compete with your partner assigning the victory to "the person who first gets the lower lip of the other."

Pressure kiss

The pressure kiss may appear aggressive, but quite a lot of people enjoy it. This kiss incorporates biting and keeping the mouth and the lips of your accomplice closed. Therefore, it is imperative to do it only briefly to don't hurt them. To keep the passion flowing, you can also make a circle with your fingers and kiss them against your partner's lips; this will also help reduce the pressure if needed.

Top kiss

This kiss produces delicious sensations, as the top kiss includes one lover kissing the upper lip of the other. While this occurs, the other accomplice can kiss the lower lip, making them tingle all over.

Distraction kiss

This kiss is mentioned in the original Kama Sutra and makes its purpose clear with only its name. It is used to draw your partner's attention, but this kiss shouldn't only be limited to the mouth. It can include other parts of the body, including the face, ear, neck, chest, and any of the erogenous zones of both the man and the woman.

Clip kiss

The clip kiss is where one partner touches the other's tongue or lips with their tongue, causing a "battle of tongues," which can be very pleasurable for both. This is a profoundly passionate type of kiss but, according to the original book, this kiss can also show immaturity.

Stirring kiss

One of the most tender and sweet kisses is the stirring kiss. One accomplice kisses the other sweetly but firmly to kindle their passion. The original Kama Sutra doesn't contain a lot of details regarding this type of kiss. It suggests a woman doing this to her lover while they are sleeping. It is a classic demonstration of love and romance.

Contact kiss

The contact kiss is perfect for a steamy sex prelude. During this kiss, one accomplice provocatively and gently touches the other's mouth with their lips, and there's light yet extraordinary contact; it is brief but exciting.

Kiss to ignite the flame

The kiss ignites the flame when one lover returns to awake the other with a kiss at night. Here is when you perceive how sexual politics have changed throughout the centuries. The original text is vague but makes us consider the importance of consent. It says the lady might want to pretend still to be asleep to "find her lover's mood."

Eyelash kiss

Those with long eyelashes love this sort of kiss from the Kamasutra; the eyelash kiss is when you caress and touch your accomplice's lips with your eyelashes.

Finger kiss

The kiss with a finger is energizing from start to finish, as one accomplice places their finger in the other's mouth, takes it out, and brushes it across their lips. This kiss makes it an ideal introduction to oral sex.

Reflecting kiss

Some kisses in the Kama Sutra can show desire and love without kissing your partner. A reflecting kiss is when you see the reflection of your partner in a mirror or in water to show how seriously you want them. This kiss is like a transferred kiss that might involve kissing a picture or a statue and transferring the love to an inanimate object. It's very similar to when teenagers kiss the posters of their idols hanging in their bedrooms.

3.3 Scratching

The art of scratching has its own section in the original Kama Sutra.
There are tons of different ways to scratch your lover and spice up your relationship. Here I am listing my interpretation of the most common scratching techniques reported in the original text.

Sounding

Sounding is a soft scratching that does not leave any marks. When a person scratches the chin, the breasts, the lower lip, or the Jaghana (the loin; the buttocks) of another so softly, it makes the partner's hair stand up. The nails themselves make a sound, called a 'sounding or pressing with the nails.'

Half Moon

This scratch leaves a curved mark with the nails that resembles a 'half-moon.' It is usually impressed on the neck and the breasts or other sensitive body parts of your partner.

Circle

A circle is made by two half-moons created beside each other. This mark with the nails is generally made on the navel, the small cavities about the buttocks, and the thigh joints.

Line

This is probably the simplest type of scratch. It is made in the shape of a small line and can be applied to any part of the body.

Tiger's Nail

A curved scratch, usually made on the breast, is called a 'tiger's nail.'

Peacock's Foot

This type of scratch requires a great deal of skill to make it properly. The 'Peacock's Foot' is a curved mark made by pressing all five nails into the breast. It requires a lot of practice to apply the same pressure with all five fingers and leave five perfect curved marks.

The Jump of a Hare

The 'Jump of a Hare' is realized when five marks with the nails are made close to one another near the nipple of the breast.

Leaf of a Blue Lotus

This mark is made in the shape of a lotus near the breast. It is designed to be placed in hidden locations across the body, particularly on the breast, so they are only seen by the two lovers and by no one else. They are there to remind their lover and excite them whenever they gaze upon each mark.

3.4 Eight Bites of Love

We discussed embraces, scratches, kisses, but what about biting?
Biting is probably one of the most exciting art explained in the Kama Sutra; if done correctly can lead your partner to immeasurable pleasure. There is a bite suitable for every situation; the important thing is to know which one.

Gudhaka

Gudhka is the lightest of bites, and it is typically applied only to the lower lip and does not leave any imprint. It is intended to be a careful bite to be used during the foreplay.

Uchhunaka

A *Uchhunaka*, or dazzled bite, usually leaves a weak imprint. This bite focuses on a famous erogenous zone, the ears. It can also be executed on the left cheek. It is not intended as a single bite; when performing the *Uchhunaka*, you want to slowly and repeatedly bite the ears of your partner while reaching with your hands the sensible areas of their body. This bite shows control, and it is typically used during the foreplay when it is almost time to move to the sexual act.

Bindu

The *Bindu* (a small speck), like the *Uchhunanka*, is an elaborate bite. Other than the ears and cheeks, the *"solitary bite"* could also be made on the brow. But, again, the lover needs to nip the skin so shrewdly that the imprint is only the size of a sesame seed.

Bindu Mala

The *Bindu Mala* are multiple bites usually made in circles on various parts of the body. Areas, where Bindu Mala can be applied, are neck, bosoms, empty of the tights. Using a *Bindu Mala* requires a lot of experience; the final goal is to create patterns resembling necklaces, bracelets, or jewelry with these marks.

Pravalamani

Pravalamani is a type of bite applied using the upper teeth or the upper incisors. The objective is to leave a little, decorative curved imprint on your partner. A *Pravalamani* mark resembles a half-moon due to the precision required to execute this type of mark. Due to the precision required, it is suggested not to perform this bite during sexual acts. Instead, use *Pravalamani* during the foreplay or in a moment of relaxation when you are still in complete control of your body.

Mani Mala

Mani Mala is very similar to the *Bindu Mala*, but in this case, the "*necklaces*" created have more extensive "*corals*" -the bite-size is slightly bigger-. The part of the body where it is used usually is breasts and tights.

Khandabhraka

Khandabhrakas are "*clouds*" of small bites scattered across the body without a particular arrangement. It is pretty common to apply these marks under the breasts, and due to the spontaneity of these patterns, this type of bite can be easily used during sexual acts.

Varaha Charvita

Varaha Charvita, also called chewing of the wild boar, is a variation of *Khandabhrakas* where the marks are closer and redder in the center. These bites are placed randomly and made in a state of great excitement during the sexual act. Compared to the other types of bites, *Varaha Charvita* and *Khandabhrakas* require less control and precision and, for this reason, are perfect to be executed during the sexual act.

3.5 Sucking the Mango Fruit: Fellatio Techniques

The Kama Sutra presents different fellatio techniques; in this chapter, I will summarize the most interesting. These can be used both during the foreplay but also are perfect for the sexual congress or the grand finale!

Touching

According to the original Kama Sutra text, touching, or *Nimitta,* is: "When your lover catches your penis in her hand and, shaping her lips to an 'O', lays them lightly to its tip, moving her head in tiny circles."

Nominal Congress

This technique is based on holding the penis in a single hand while placing your lips on it. The only -slow- movement is done with your mouth and tongue, and the focus is mainly on the gland.

Biting the Sides

With this technique, your fingers are used to cover the gland and slowly massage it while you then kiss and bite along the shaft.

Kissing

This is just a warmup technique where you hold the penis in the hand while covering it in kisses.

Rubbing

Remarkably like kissing, this occurs when you use your tongue and lick all over the penis until it is fully erected.

Sucking a Mango Fruit

Putting only half of the penis in the mouth and sucking on it

Swallowing Up

This is when the entire penis is placed in the mouth and down towards the back of the throat.

Outer Pincers

With this technique, you take the head of the penis gently between your lips, by turns pressing, kissing it tenderly, and pulling at its soft skin: this is "*Bahiha-Samdansha*" (the Outer Pincers).

Inner Pincers

This is the follow-up of the Outer Pincers technique. You allow the head to slide entirely into your mouth and press the shaft firmly between your lips, holding a moment before pulling away; it is called "*Antaha-Samdansha*" (the Inner Pincers).

3.6 Let Your Senses Evolve

During the demonstration of lovemaking, a considerable lot of us will zero in on just the feeling of touch. We are distracted, essentially, by what adoring our accomplices feels like.

Yet shouldn't something be said about the other senses. What are you seeing? While the feeling of touch is so alive during our sexual experiences, what we see is likewise loaded with enchantment. Our accomplices are wonderlands of creaturely magnificence. We need to recognize the truth about that and add it to our sensual collection. As they burn through our accomplices with appreciation, our eyes are an under-used sense in the actual domain of the faculties – sexuality. You might think that men are more visual than ladies; experience has instructed me that this is not the case. Ladies have similarly a strong enthusiasm for what they see as men do. Men may locate this hard to accept, yet ladies' eyes see you for the sexy animals you are!

Our feeling of smell is overwhelmingly significant because it plays in causing us to select our partners. Even if we are not even aware of it, pheromones influence what attracts us to each other. The pheromonal aroma does not enroll with us, however, in a conscious way. What does, is the exceptional aroma of our accomplices the fragrance their skin conveys, and, in any event, when vigorously perfumed, this aroma can be distinguished. This is the reason we sniff their pillows when they are away from us. This peculiar fragrance is such a lot of a piece of those we share our love with that reminds us of them and the love we share with them. In sex, this scent can have a significant impact on desire and passion, as the action of our chemicals is increased and drive passion.

Suppose you are interested in exploring your senses further. In that case, the chapter "Sensory deprivation" of this book will contain more details and ideas on how you can enhance your senses during sex.

Chapter 4: The Third Stage of Lovemaking - Sexual Congress

It is time to get down to business. The first, and most significant thing, that should be done before you get physically involved with your partner is relaxing. Following a long, stressful day at work, you need to loosen up both your body and your brain. It would help if you left your troubles behind. Relaxing is very subjective; it can be accomplished in different ways. It is up to you discovering what works for your body and mind. This can be a hot shower, a snooze, or a run. By setting aside the effort to unwind before getting private with your accomplice, you are guaranteeing that you will not be diverted contemplating your day while you are with your partner. As previously mentioned, preparation and foreplay are equally important. Take your time, and do not rush towards sex! Once you feel both ready, then it is time to get down to business!

In this chapter, I have collected some of the most exciting sex positions of the Kama Sutra. Some of them might be pretty complex and require flexibility that not everyone has. My suggestion is to try some of these positions you find interesting and see which are the best for you.

4.1 Sex Positions

1. Sammukha

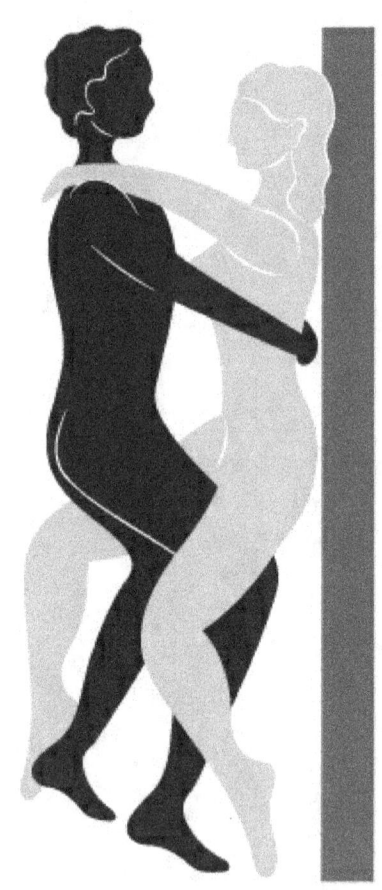

Difficulty: Medium

Description: *The Sammukha* is a moderately simple position to begin with and one you have likely never thought to attempt. Your accomplice leans back against a wall in this position while spreads their legs as wide as possible while you penetrate them. If your partner is shorter, they may need to stand on a footrest or something similar to find a comfortable position.

2. Janukurpara

Difficulty: Hard

Description: Sex standing up gets negative criticism; however, trust me, the *Janukurpara* position is fantastic since it offers extra-deep penetration and loads of eye contact. In this position, you lift your accomplice, locking your elbows under their knees and gripping their butt with your hands while they place their arms around your neck.

3. Piditaka

Difficulty: Medium

Description: After some glorious failures, I have learned that acrobatic sex does not always equate to pleasurable sex. The *Piditaka* position is a relaxed, laid-back position that has the advantage of being amazingly delightful. In this position, your accomplice lies on their back and pulls their knees into their chest, laying their feet on your chest as you kneel before them. With your knees on both sides of their hips, you raise their hips onto your thighs and penetrate them.

4. Virsha (Reverse cowgirl)

Difficulty: Easy

Description: The *Virsha* position is commonly known as "the Reverse Cowgirl." In this position, the male lies on his back while his accomplice sits or kneels on top of him, facing his feet. The woman, at that point, brings down themselves onto you and leans forward, grasping the male's lower legs.

5. Tripadam (The ballet dancer)

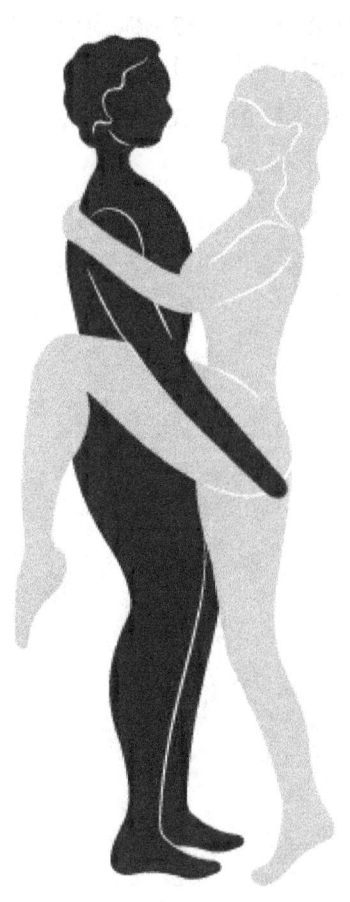

Difficulty: Medium

Description: In this position, you both stand, facing each other. The male puts his hand under one of his accomplice's knees and raises it off the floor, transforming the couple into a "*Tripadam*"(or tripod). At that point, the male is in a perfect position to start the penetration.

This position is perfect for some quick sex, it does not allow for deep penetration, but it is terrific if you want to keep a high pace. *Tripadan* works best if both of you are around a similar height.

6.Indrani

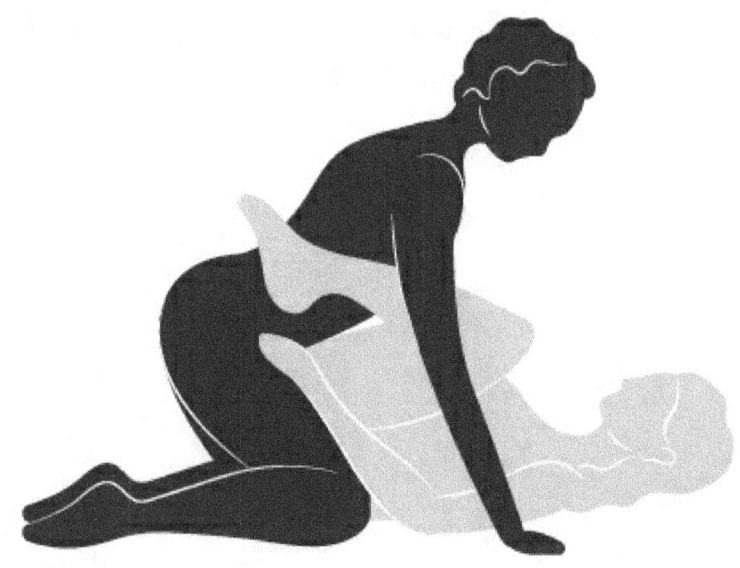

Difficulty: Easy

Description: *Indrani* is named for the beautiful and alluring spouse of Indra, the incomparable god in the Hindu faith. With this position, your accomplice lies on their back and pulls their knees into their chest. Your knees can ride your accomplice's hips, so you have your hands allowed to stimulate their body, or you can be on your lower arms.

7. Butterfly

Diffculty: Medium

Description: In this position, the partners are facing each other. The man is on the bottom while the woman can give the pace. The *Butterfly* allows for deep penetration, and once the couple has found the right balance, it is possible to keep a high speed if desired or enjoy deep and slow penetrations.

8. Utphallaka

Difficulty: Easy

Description: *Utphallaka* is also known as blossoming. In this position, the woman lies down on her back, resting her head on the bed. She raises her hips and wraps her legs around her partner. This position allows easy penetration since both partners are on the same level, and the genitals of the receiving partner are easily accessible.

9. Parshva samputa

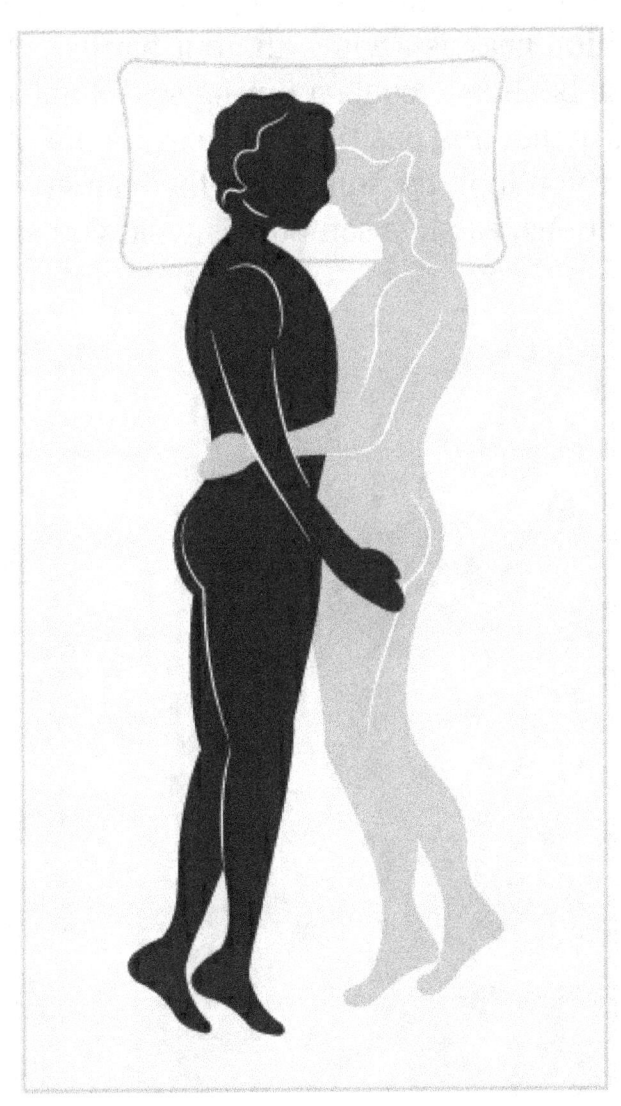

Difficulty: Easy

Description: *Parshva Samputa* is also called a lateral box. The main challenge of this position is a vis-à-vis with your partner. You must lie down face to face and do not break eye contact during sex. Some people find it hard to handle the proximity that this position enforces, while others enjoy it very much. Give it a try! If you look for something that can give you a break from more challenging positions, parshva samputa is what you are looking for.

10. Uttana samputa

Difficulty: Easy

Description: This position is a variation of *Parshva Samputa* called also closed box. *Uttana Samputa* is also harder than its predecessor since the woman is lying down, stretched out, with the man on the top of her, pressing into her hips.

11. Padmasana (The lotus)

Diffculty: Medium

Description: *Padmasana* is remarkably like the yoga lotus position. The man is seated with his legs crossed while the woman is on the top with her legs around her partner's torso. As you can imagine, *Padmasana* requires a good level of flexibility to enjoy it fully. I have personally tried this position multiple times, and it is impressive once you find the right fit between your bodies.

12. Jrimbhitaka

Difficulty: Medium

Description: In this position, the lady raises her legs and puts them on her accomplice's shoulders; in this way, her knees are locked over his shoulders. Jrimbhitaka allows deep penetration, and it's perfect when used for slow and long sex.

13. Magic mountain

Difficulty: Easy

Description: The *Magic Mountain* position is one of the relaxing positions of the Kama Sutra. The woman lies on her front and props herself up on her elbows. The partner kneels behind her to penetrate the woman from behind. He can also use his hands to hold her waist or stimulate her body during the act.

14. The good ex

Difficulty: Medium

Description: The *Good Ex* is a medium-level difficulty position. The couple sits on the bed facing each other with legs forward. Lift your accomplice's right leg over your left and lift your right leg over your partner's left. Come closer so the male can start the penetration. Once you are locked in this position, lie back with your legs forming an X. Then male can slowly begin the penetration.

15. The Pinball Wizard

Difficulty: Hard

Description: For this position, the woman must form a bridge with all her weight resting on her shoulders. The male can then penetrate her from a kneeling position. This position is excellent for the woman since it allows the male to have easy access to the clitoris and, in general, her entire body; he can then provide additional stimulation.

16. Cowgirl's Helper

Difficulty: Easy

Description: This ideal first-time position, Cowgirl, is another name for sex with the man on his back and the lady on top riding him. It lets her set the pace and the angle of penetration as she pleases. At the same time, the man gets a phenomenal view and has access to almost all the partner's body. This can be used to provide additional stimulation during the sex act.

17. Stand and Deliver

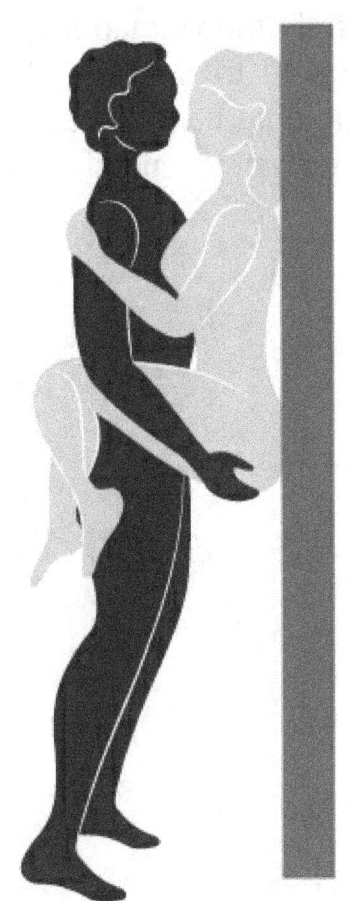

Difficulty: Hard

Description: *Stand and Deliver* is a physically challenging position. The man must bear almost entirely the woman's weight while she leans on a wall. Once the right angle is found to improve stability, she can wrap her legs around the partner while holding her back against the hips. This is a position that is hard to maintain for an extended period but lets you spend a few minutes in heaven!

18. Pretzel Dip

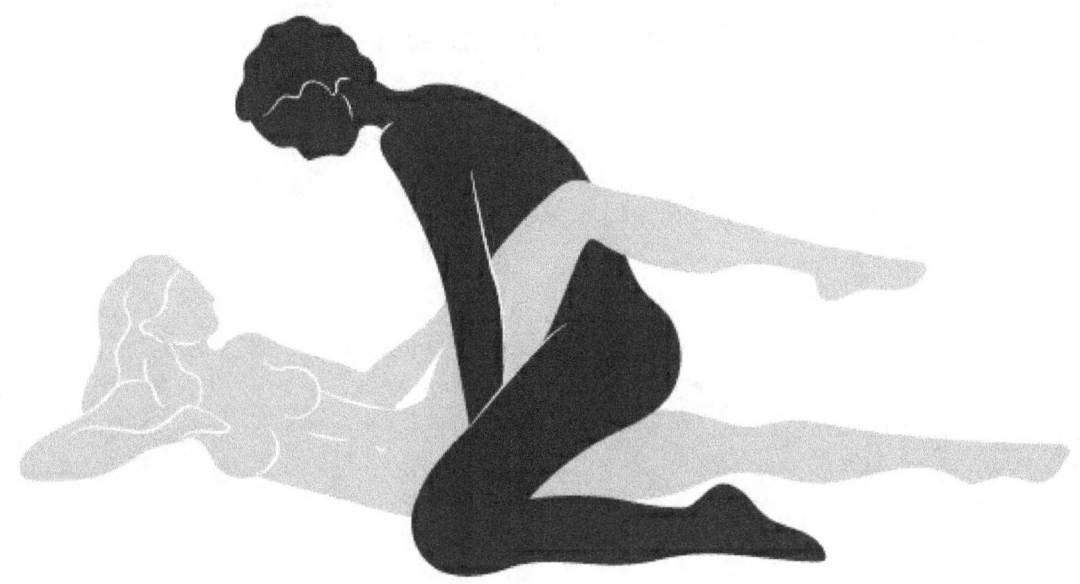

Difficulty: Easy

Description: The *Pretzel Dip* is one of the lazy positions in Kama Sutra; the woman has to lie on her side and relax. Meanwhile, the man must kneel and straddle the partner's right leg while lifting her left to be curled around their left side. You can get good deep penetration in this position, remarkably like the doggy style but without breaking the eye contact. Also, since the man has his hands free, he can be creative and make good use of them.

19. Butter Churner

Difficulty: Hard

Description: This position requires a good level of flexibility of the woman. She has to lie on her back with her legs raised and folded over, so her ankles are on one or the other side of her head, while the male squats and starts the penetration.

20. Seated Wheelbarrow

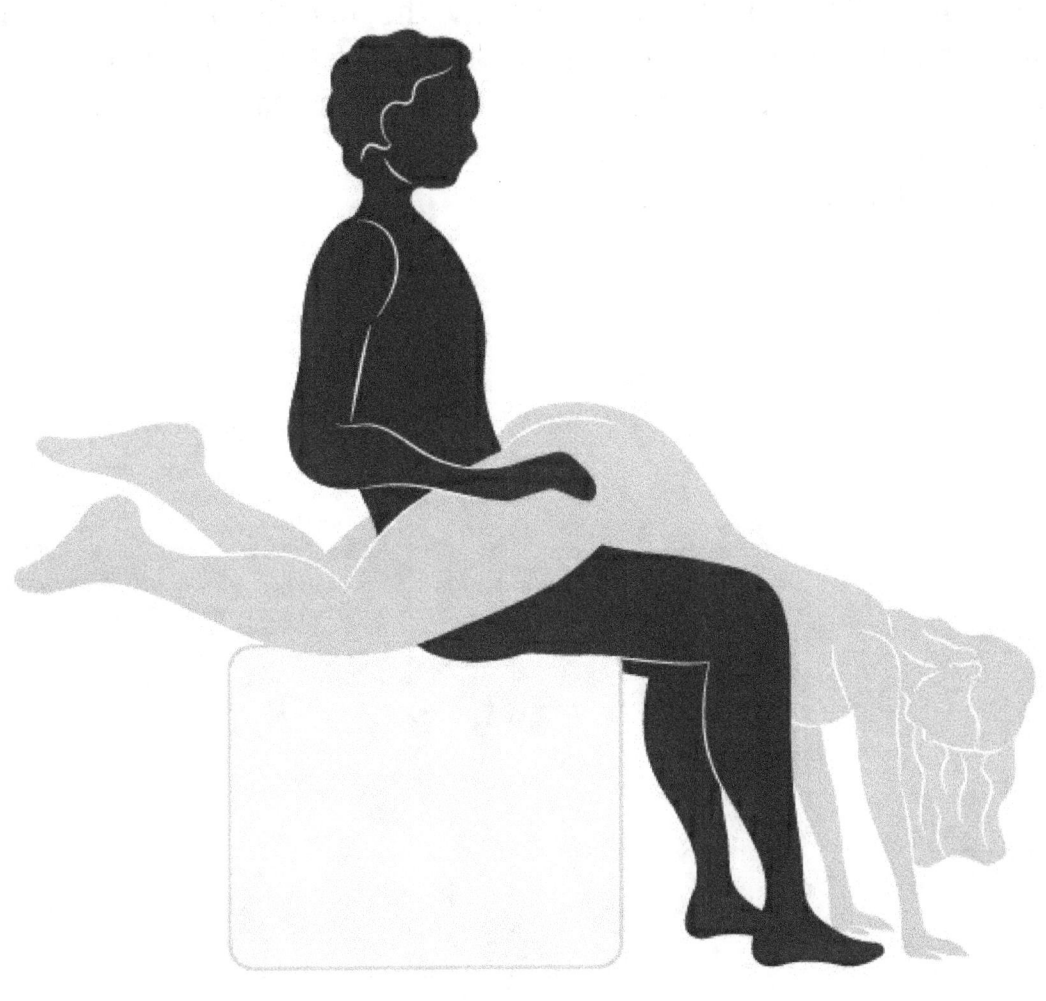

Difficulty: Medium

Description: In the seated wheelbarrow, the man sits on the bed while the woman gets down on her front as the partner starts the penetration. The man lifts the woman by the pelvis while the lady grips the partner around the waist with her legs. This position is a more accessible version of the standing wheelbarrow, but it has its challenges.

21. Arc de Triomphe

Difficulty: Medium

Description: In this position, your partner has to extend his legs while sitting on the bed. When he is in place, crawl up to him on your knees and ride his erect penis while you arch your back, as shown in the image. Don't arc too much, and try to respect the natural flexibility of your body. In this position, you can rest your head on his legs and grab his ankles for better stability.

22. Supernova

Difficulty: Easy

Description: In this position, the man leans on his back on the bed while the woman rides him, as shown in the image. The upper back of the man has to lean outside the bad arching towards the floor. In this position, the woman is in complete control, and because the man's head is upside down, he will experience a blood rush, making him experience what is called "erotic inversion." Although the orgasms that men can experience in this position are totally different, they will love it.

23. Spread Eagle

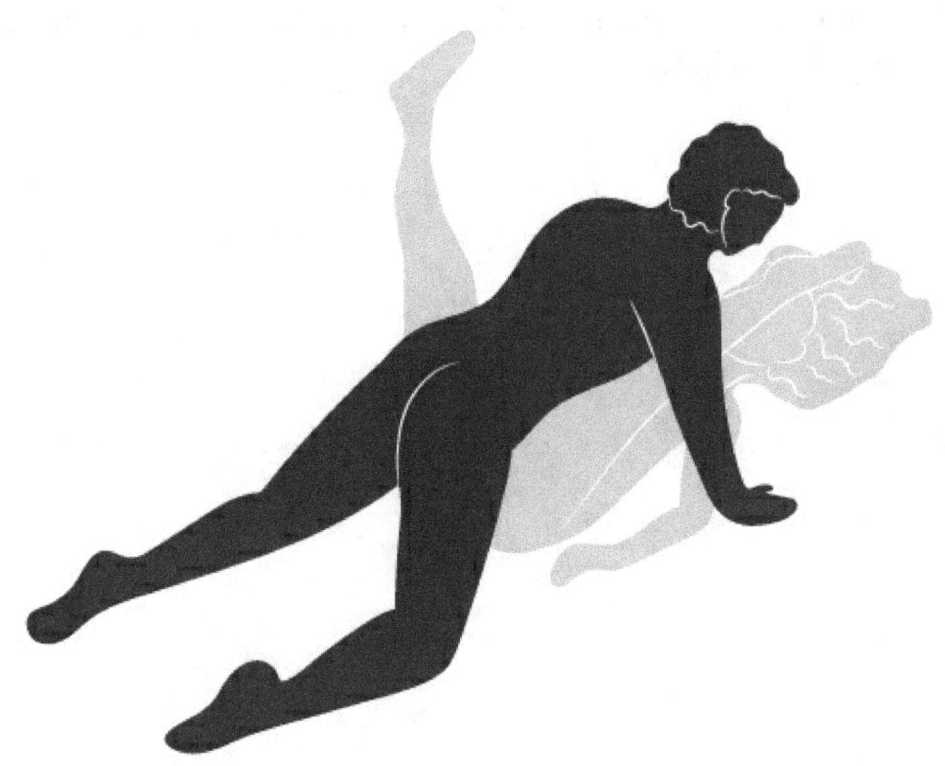

Difficulty: Medium

Description: To try this position, you might need some warm-up stretches first since it requires the woman to show some flexibility. Starting from the missionary position, the woman can raise her legs and extend them straight out (forming a "V" shape). This small change to missionary position allows for deeper penetration. If you struggle with stability, the woman could try to grab her ankles to find a better balance and lock her legs in position.

24. Chairman

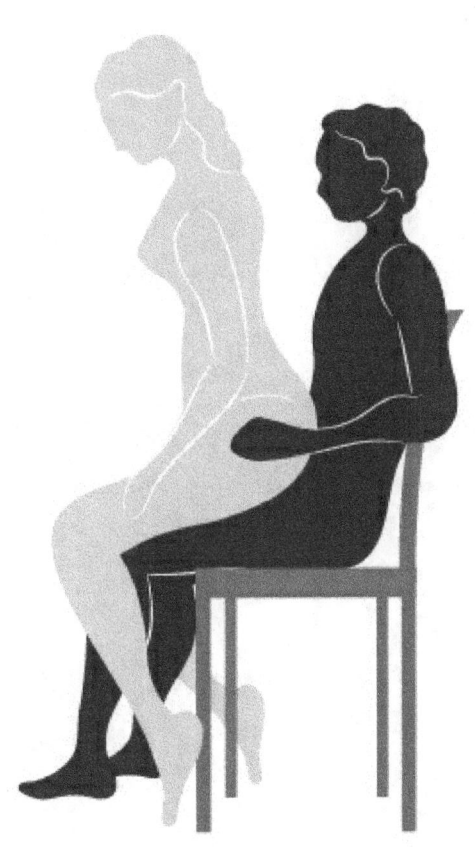

Difficulty: Easy

Description: This position is fantastic to reach the G-Spot effortlessly. Also, the hands of both partners are free and can provide extra stimulation. I believe the Chairman doesn't require a long description; the man sits on a chair, and the woman rides him, controlling the pace and angle of penetration.

25. Wheelbarrow

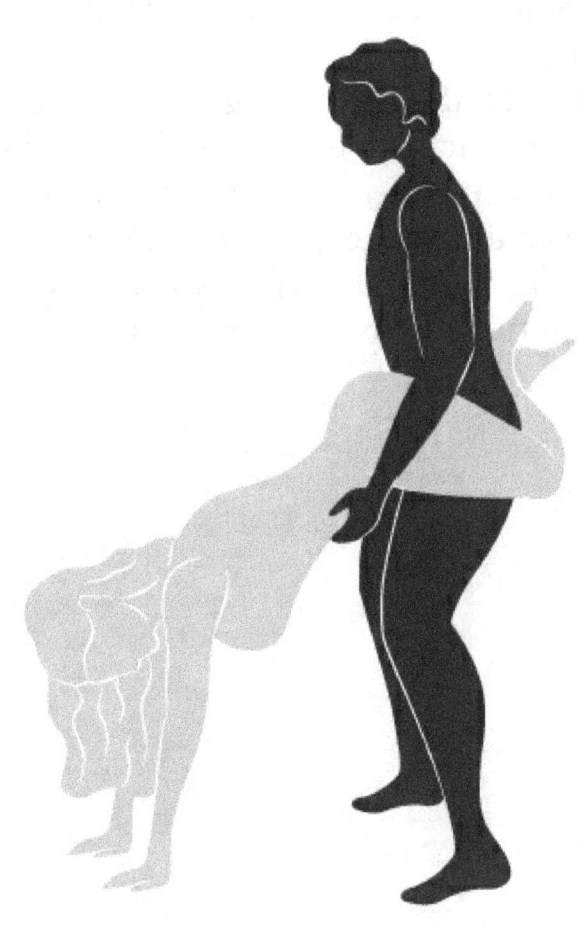

Difficulty: Hard

Description: This position requires some upper-body strenght for both partners and good stability. Also, it takes a little finessing to get the right penetration angle. However, you can hit those hard-to-reach erogenous zones (G-Spot included) trying new incredible sensations with the Wheelbarrow position.

The giving partner stands with the legs slightly open, and the knees bent. First, the receiving partner should bend over, placing the hands on the floor. Next, the giving partner will raise the receiving partner's legs to help lock them in position while guiding the initial penetration.

Once you are in alignment, the giving partner can start the thrusting motion adjusting from time to time the angle of penetration.

4.2 Improve missionary sex

Most of the time, having sex, the man inserts the penis and starts a rhythmic movement in and out. This does not sound particularly exciting; luckily, there are many other less tedious ways to orgasm for both of you! If you do not feel like venturing into complex sexual positions in this section of the book, I will explain how to get maximum pleasure from a simple position like the missionary.

Churning

With this technique, we want to take advantage of the different sensitivities of the vaginal walls. Grab your penis at the base, and once inserted, start making circular movements inside the vagina. This will allow you to stimulate areas that you would hardly reach with an in and out motion and, in this way, discover the most sensitive points.

Rubbing

With this technique, we want to try something different. Usually, to achieve maximum vaginal stimulation, it is recommended to focus on the front vaginal wall, where the G-Spot is located. Most women love this type of stimulation, but everyone is different. With rubbing, we want to reach the backside of the vagina and unleash completely different sensations. Once you have assumed the missionary position, perform the penetration in a downward motion instead of the expected upward movement. When performing this type of stimulation, it is essential to keep the penetration short and sharp at a brisk pace. A well-executed rubbing will trigger a gamma of completely different sensations in your partner!

Piercing

This technique has the characteristic of improving clitoral stimulation and is based on slightly changing your position. The woman should put her hips slightly lower while the man aligns his shoulders with the partner's head. Thrusting in and out in this position will increase clitoral stimulation; you will both love it!

Buffeting

Try to penetrate your partner all way in and out. When you are almost out, penetrate in again with a fast hard stroke. This move has a primitive, practically animal-like feel, and many women find it incredibly arousing.

Boar's blow

With this technique, we want to stimulate the lateral vaginal walls. Some research has shown that one side of the clitoris is almost always more sensitive than the other; it is therefore not absurd to think that this could be valid for different areas. When in missionary position, penetrate your partner at a brisk pace trying to use a slightly tilted motion to the right or left.

Sporting of a Sparrow

This technique is based on the fact that the initial part of the vagina is the most sensitive for many women. Use short and quick penetrations to stimulate this area, letting your partner guide your pace and depth of the penetration.

4.3 Beyond the G-Spot

This section is a more modern addition to the traditional Kama Sutra. At the time, in fact, the knowledge of human anatomy was not as advanced as today; even if the existence of various erogenous zones was already known, the most recent research has shown that the G-Spot is not the only hot area to focus on for thundering orgasms. Experts still disagree, but it looks like there are other four potential "spots," called deep vaginal erogenous zones, that may be at least as sensitive as the G-Spot.

The A-Spot

This spot is found on the front vaginal wall just before the cervix. Slowly move your finger in the area until you feel some *"divots"* on both sides. Then move inside an inch or two to locate the perfect spot.

To awaken the A-Spot, you need to apply some pressure or move your finger; touch is not enough to stimulate the vagina. The best way to stimulate this area is to use a move called "anchor and pull." Place the padded part of your finger on the a-spot and gently pull it towards you; you will immediately notice if you are making the right moves based on your partner's reaction.

The O-Spot

Only 8% of the women are sensitive here, and you could be one of the lucky ones! To find the O-Spot, you must locate the G-Spot first.

You can refer to this diagram to locate it.

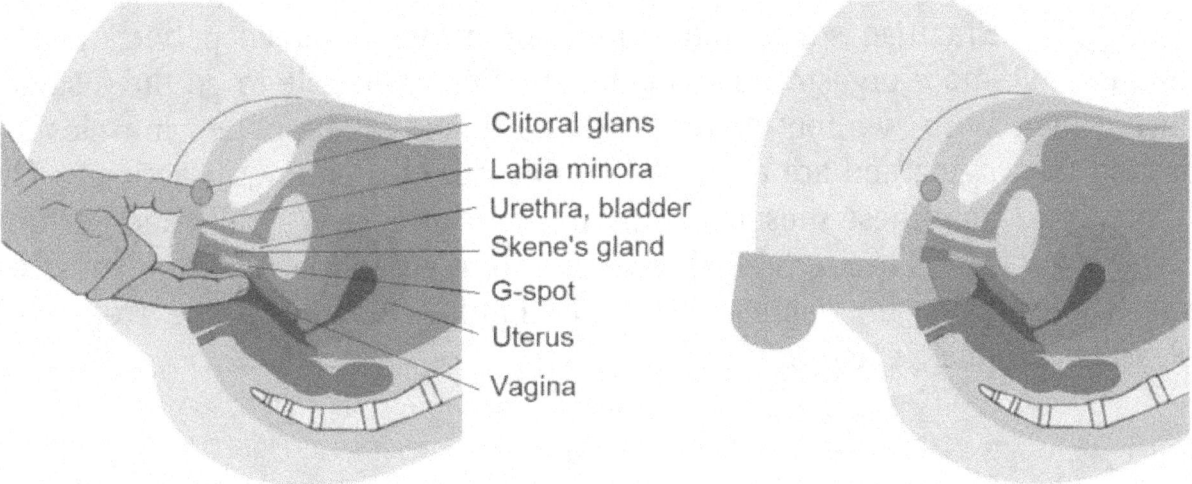

(Source: Pfaus, Quintana, Mac Cionnath, Parada: The whole versus the sum of some of the parts: toward resolving the apparent controversy of clitoral versus vaginal orgasms. In: Socioaffective Neuroscience & Psychology, 2016)

The bulbs of vestibule surrounding the vaginal orifice can't be shown in this sagittal section.

Once the G-Spot is found, then rotate your finger on the opposite vaginal wall and go deeper until you reach a spongy area; this is the O-Spot. The sensations your partner will feel when stimulated in this area will be remarkably like what she would experience with anal sex. The best stimulation can be achieved by using the "anchor and pull" technique on the G-Spot and O-Spot simultaneously. To do that, you will require to use both hands together, with one palm facing up and the other facing down. This position will allow the index fingers to reach both areas at the same time.

Cervical orgasm

It is estimated that only 7.5% of women have ever experienced a cervical orgasm. When the woman becomes aroused, the cervix lifts, but it is still possible to reach it. The most effective stimulation of the cervix is obtained during ovulation, which is usually placed between day 13 and day 16 of the cycle. You can use two fingers to stimulate it, making small circles on the cervix and slowly applying some pressure. Your partner will begin to feel a pleasure that involves the whole body. If you have difficulty reaching the cervix, you can help yourself with a sufficiently long vibrator. Trust me; it will be worth it!

Pelvic muscles

A 2014 Brazilian study found that women with trained pelvic muscles tend to have more orgasms. The main reason is to be able to go the distance during intercourse without getting tired so quickly. The pelvic muscles are around the vagina and are easily accessible but challenging to activate. The best way to train these muscles is to buy a set of Ben Wa balls and perform Kegel exercises. These "vaginal weights" are great to tone up those muscles, and if kept inside the vagina, they can stimulate other sensitive areas with pleasant and unexpected results.

4.4 Sex positions to overcome anxiety and insecurity

Anxiety and insecurity in bed are not easy to overcome; in some cases, if they start to impact your sex life negatively, resorting to a specialist could be the most appropriate choice. There is no magic formula to permanently solve these problems other than a lot of work on yourself, but some positions can help you feel more comfortable than others. This section contains some tips to mitigate the sense of anxiety and insecurity that pervades you during sexual intercourse.

Best Positions to Try on the off chance that you are Insecure

Using a seated position can instill a sense of security and make you feel less exposed and vulnerable during sexual intercourse.

In this first position, the man will sit in the seat, and the woman can ride him looking him straight in the eye. This position ensures a sense of control for the person on top who can decide the pace and depth of the penetration. This comfortable position gives a sense of safety since you will face the person you trust, and your bodies will be firmly wrapped together. The feeling of closeness and intimacy with your partner should be able to calm your insecurities and allow you to enjoy the moment.

Alternatively, you can try a more classic position in bed, **lying face to face with your partner**. This time the woman should position herself slightly higher than her partner, with one of her legs used to wrap the partner's hips. In this position, the penetration is not complex, and the hips drive all the action. Bonding with your partner and lying face to face together should instill a sense of security and foster communication. <u>Ideally, any sexual position that allows you to face your partner and promotes a large contact area between your bodies will naturally instill confidence.</u>

Eye-to-eye connection is critical. In addition, the capacity to kiss and touch your accomplice is additionally significant. Along these lines, when you search for positions that will lessen your weakness, it is ideal to pick ones where you are confronting each other.

Best Sex Positions for Anxious Lovers

Having tension about sex is not unprecedented. There are numerous causes for feeling anxious about sex, some rational, some less so.

There is a wide range of sex positions that you can try that will help decrease the degree of tension you are encountering. Also, being open and speaking with your accomplice about how you are feeling is vital to get rid of this negative energy.

One of the recommended postures to combat performance anxiety is called "**associated hearts**," which is remarkably like the cowgirl style. In this position, the man is initially lying on his back while the woman rides him. At this point, the man, using his arms, raises his torso, getting near the partner and precisely bringing the hearts getting near closer. This position guarantees eye-to-eye contact and, at the same time, a reasonable degree of intimacy helpful in relaxing and chasing away negative thoughts. If this position does not help, you could try the variant in which the woman is turned, and the man comes into contact with her back.

Sometimes, the tension can be caused by the partner's stares and feelings during intercourse; if you think you fit into this group, you may want to try positions with minimal eye contact.

Doggie style is another excellent position when you are feeling tension. It allows a decent measure of contact, yet you will not need to glance at each other in the face. During the doggie style, the man's vision is pleasant while the woman can concentrate on the sensations and eventually close her eyes and let go.

Chapter 5: The Fourth Stage of Lovemaking – After Play

Afterplay is the last stage of lovemaking, and it is often neglected. Many couples prefer to conclude with the sexual act and avoid potentially embarrassing moments in bed. In my opinion, the after play is as important as the other parts, and it is a special moment that can reinforce the relationship and lead to more fantastic sex.

Yet, what is after play? In a real sense, it implies what you do after you play (i.e., engage in sexual relations). While normal post-coital activities incorporate nodding off, going after your telephone, or in any event, leaving the space to continue ahead with your day or night, there are other activities that you can do as a couple. After play does not need to last ages. Even only a couple of minutes of closeness will do; being together just after sex helps couples feel less void after a particularly private act – as would be the situation if one of you dismisses after you're finished.

You have probably noticed that men are more likely to nod off not long after they have intercourse, otherwise known as no after play at all, yet you should not be angry with your accomplice for doing this since he, in a real sense, cannot resist. There are many potential biochemical and evolutionary reasons for post-sex sleepiness, but no one has pinpointed the exact causes. In this chapter, I will show some ideas for after play in the hope of inspiring the couples that would like to spend more time with their partner and at the same time avoid the "collapse effect" of their partner.

5.1 Pillow Talk

Talk after sex is an excellent way to reinforce the relationship, share feelings and become closer as a couple. You don't need to say romantic things; this is just an ideal chance to reveal to one another how you feel. Furthermore, on the off chance that you have been together for quite a while, it's an excellent chance to talk about whatever you want, share your emotions, and remind each other that you are a team! If you are both open-minded and relaxed, you could even direct an after-death analysis (in a sexy way, obviously) of your sex meeting. You can select the pieces you loved most and what you might want to attempt sometime later or require improvements. The important thing is that you understand you can get good value from your time spend doing pillow talk.

5.2 Kiss Each Other

It might seem obvious, but kissing is another way to conclude a fantastic evening; enlarge this concept, maybe involving a few more relaxed Kama sutra kisses from the chapters before. If you still feel playful, this might be the beginning of the second round!

5.3 A Romantic Shower

Another idea to close the evening could be to take a shower together.

In the event that you both need to clean up after your sex meeting (all around done on getting so hot and hot!), why not do so together in the shower? It prolongs the intimacy you shared during sex, and if you add stimulating props like fragrant healing candles or shower salts, it could make it similarly as sexy as well.

5.4 Cuddling together

Try not to hurry to unravel after you've both arrived at the end goal. Stay folded over one another and kiss and nestle for a piece. Delicate, non-sexual kisses are best as, even though it's OK on the off chance that it prompts Round Two, that isn't the objective of after play. Indeed, even lying together clasping hands is great as maintain physical contact is.

5.5 Enjoy a chuckle

Offer a joke or essentially make each other snicker. Chuckling together is a fast and straightforward approach to bond with your accomplice. Also, if your after-sex shine by one way or another is not sufficient, snickering together will put a major grin all over as well. This is a way to show that your relationship can go beyond physical attraction and make your partner understand that eventually, you will be there to laugh together and enjoy the moment.

Also, a good laugh and some chat can give you time to recharge the batteries and start the second round.

Chapter 6: Ideas to Improve Your Sex Life

There are hundreds of different angles from which you can approach your sensuality. Here I will list some of the most common fetishes, "perversions," toys, and ideas.

As you will probably notice as you continue reading, most of these ideas were not included in the original Kama Sutra. What I am showing in this chapter is much more modern but still based on the same principles. You might already be familiar with all of them or not, but this may be the perfect time to make your list. Discuss with your partner what you both like and what intrigues you. The thing you need to remember is that there are no taboos in a relationship. If all the parties involved are in agreement, there are no limits to what can be experienced together. Do not be afraid to try with your partner any of these; you may discover, much to your surprise, a new side of your relationship.

Before we start, I would like to introduce the concept of fetishes. The expression "*fetish*" may inspire pictures of dark leather bodysuits and convoluted sexual contraptions; however, you may as of now be showcasing the absolute most normal models, for example, punishing. However, what characterizes a fetish is not what the action or object of want is to such an extent as the job it plays in somebody's day-to-day existence. "A fetish is commonly alluded to as conduct that somebody can't get sexually stimulated without. Fetishes can likewise be a term people use to portray a sexual excitement that is combined with a commonly non-sexual article," says sexologist and therapist Dense Renye. There are tons of different fetishes that you could try; I will list some of them in the following paragraphs.

6.1 Being vocal in the bedroom

If you are having sex in complete silence, you are not alone. This section will take a gander at how you can be more vocal during sex without feeling awkward.

Many couples do not communicate sufficiently during sex, making the experience both confusing and sometimes frustrating. Many people complain that their partner is dead silent, and they have no idea what is going on in their head.

The first thing to remember is that dirty talking is not mandatory. That said, being communicative is much more fun and constructive. If you do not talk in bed, your partner will hardly know if you liked something or not. All people have insecurities when they have sex; having a communicative person by your side can incredibly improve sexual performance. When you feel appreciated, you give more!

It is essential to create a safe environment where you can express yourself without fear and without keeping anything inside

Many people do not make a sound during intercourse for fear of saying the wrong thing and ruining the moment. I can assure you that if the person next to you supports you, you have nothing to fear.

Start alone

One of the best ways to start being more vocal in bed is to start being vocal when alone; try it during masturbation, it might sound weird, but it works. In bed, you do not need to make a speech. You can start with a few moans and slowly gain confidence. Simple phrases like "yeah, it feels good" or "I like that" can be a good starting point to get out of the shell.

Welcome weirdness

You must accept that you will not sound like a porn star overnight. At first, it will seem strange to you; getting out of your comfort zone is difficult for anyone. You will probably say embarrassing things sooner or later that will make you smile or blush. This is the best way to learn, don't give up, and keep trying; if you can take the "failures" with the proper sense of humor, I assure you that your chemistry will dramatically improve.

What you like

The most direct feedback you can give to your partner is to tell them what you like. At first, you can say what you like or when you want more of a particular thing. In this way, your feedback will always be positive and help your partner better understand your preferences.

Sound like Daft Punk

"Faster," "Slower," "Softer," "Harder." Even using a few words, you can give helpful feedback to your partner and be more involved in the action!

Be your true self

In a relationship, you should express yourself freely and say what you want in bed. You must not be ashamed of who you are and what you want. Do you want your partner to dress up like a sailor moon while making love? Would you like to lick your partner's body sprinkled with chocolate? Your partner may disagree with you, but that shouldn't stop you from expressing your deepest desires.

6.2 Roleplay

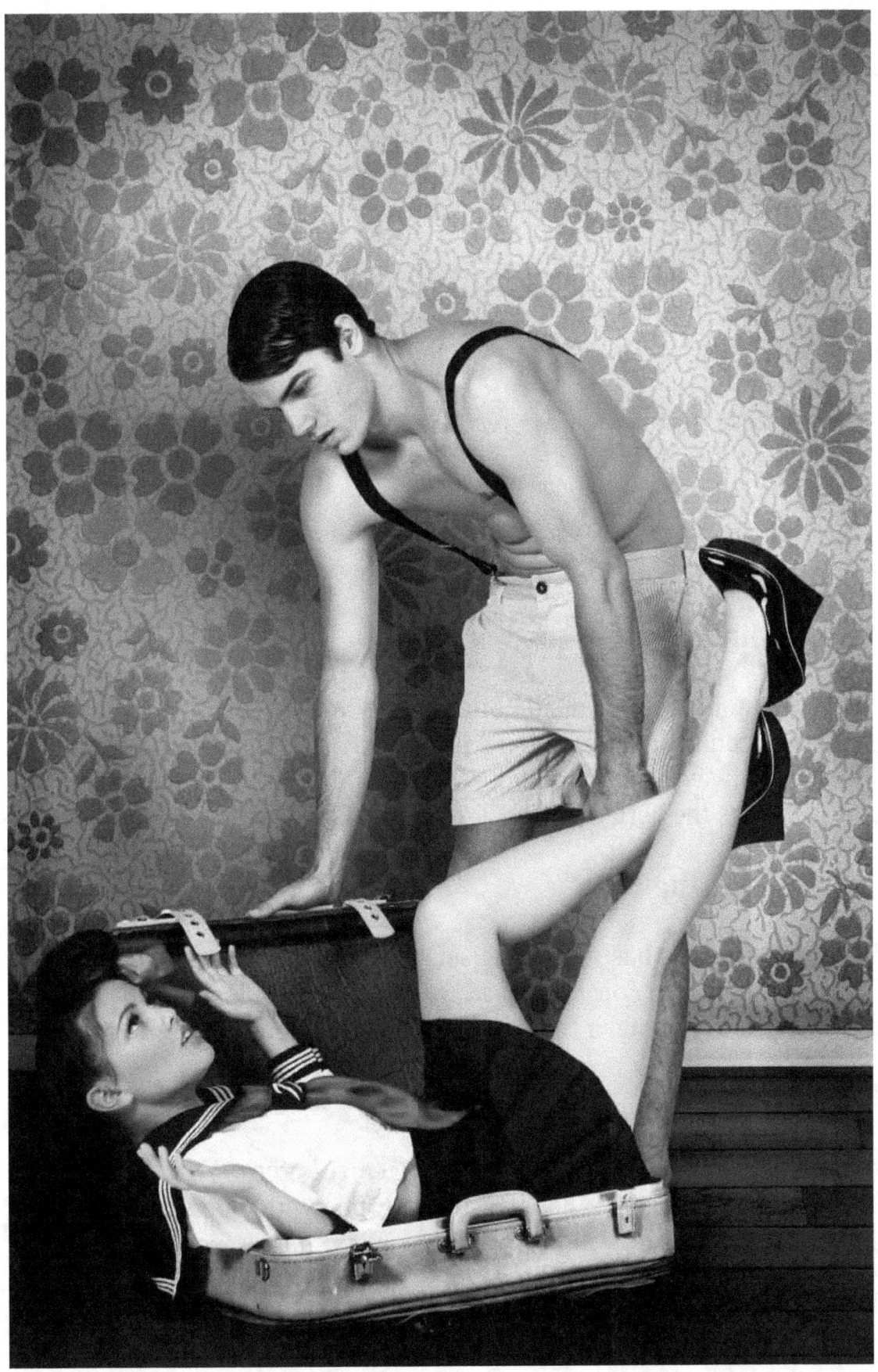

You do not need to quit playing pretends when you grow up. Acting implies showcasing a sexual dream with your partner(s), either once or as a component of a continuous dream. While it tends to be a fetish or crimp inside itself, it is additionally a solid method to carry on different dreams. For example, if you have a clinical fantasy and are excited by specialists, you presumably don't need your PCP to get sexy with you since that would be dreadful and oppressive.

Here some ideas and scenarios that you could play with your partner.

Boss and employee

This is perfect if you want to create some power dynamics. Decide who wants to be the boss (power position) and the employee (submissive role). The dressing is relatively easy, pick some clothes that are slightly sexy, and you would wear them in an office. In this scenario, you might want to have sex on a table or a desk to better channel the office vibes.

Maid or butler

Why not play the role of maid/butler and serve your partner some tea? A maid's uniform can heat up the room very quickly. If you are not a tea person well, you can always supervise house cleaning. When the maid uses the ladder, it is always the perfect opportunity to peek under her skirt.

The massage therapist

Massaging a person has something sensual about it; what about a massage with a happy ending? You will need just a few towels and oils to start playing. Also, I love to add a few candles to set the mood.

Hello stranger

Let's pretend you and your partner never met before. Your partner will approach you as a stranger. When it's the first time with a person, everything is different. The passion is more vigorous, everything is new, and there is always that bit of fear that something can go wrong. You are two people who do not know each other's names to jump into bed together. It is just sex!

Let's play the doctor

In my opinion, every scenario that involves an authority figure is super-hot, especially if this authority figure is a doctor and can touch you everywhere! For this scenario, you will only need a sexy doctor's or nurse's outfit. Give your partner a medical examination, and I am sure you will find something to double-check in the genital area.

Yoga class

Do not worry; everyone can make a yoga roleplay work. You do not require to be super flexible, but it helps. You can go pro trying exotic and sexy positions or pretend you are a novice and asks for advice from the "yoga master." As a bonus, this is also an interesting scenario if you want to try some of the most challenging sex positions of the Kama Sutra.

I'm your Queen / I'm your King

Monarchy is sexy! You will feel the power when you order your servant to reveal his "scepter." This scenario might require some costumes, but if you want to keep it simple, you can pick a comfortable armchair that will become your throne for the evening.

Professor and student

This is probably one of the most fantasized situations. Professors are one of the first authoritative figures we meet in our life, and they have their charm. You can be the naughty student who must be punished with the ruler or the horny professor who wants to seduce their student. I am personally a fan of the Japanese school's uniform for these scenarios, but you can pick your style.

Stripper and customer

It is time to dress in your sexiest clothes and move that ass. Your partner can bring some money to make it more interesting; a private dance is expensive! Do not forget some music, and if you find something that resembles a stripper pole, well...bingo!

Mistress and slave

Dominate your man with some harsh words and your whip. Leather clothes and corsets are perfect for this type of scenario, but if you do not have anything suitable in your wardrobe, a good pair of boots will help set the scene. In this scenario, you want to control and punish your partner. Agree upfront your limits and a secret word that can be used to interrupt the game at any time. Also, you might consider switching roles and become a master and slave.

6.3 Tease and denial

If the core of your sexual activity is getting naked and have ordinary sex, you might want to try this. Tease and denial games have the purpose of increasing the sensual tension, making you feel in charge while your partner will beg for more (or vice versa).

The core idea is elementary; you want to tease your partner very close to the orgasm and deny them. You want to do this repeatedly until your partner can not take it anymore and will explode in one of the most powerful orgasms they ever experienced.

Does this sound silly? Trust me when I tell you my man had some of the most unforgettable orgasms of his life with this practice, and he always came back for more.

I will not give you a play-by-play guide on how to tease your partner but just some ideas. I think the most important thing when making love is to use your creativity. You know better than I what your partner might like or dislike.

Show him what he is missing

Carefully select your outfit; it must be sexy but not show too much.
You could improvise a lap dance but do not allow him to touch! Instead, drive him crazy, slowly revealing what he is missing until he begs to have more.

You can touch, but he cannot! Now and then, I prefer to use handcuffs to make sure that the "no-touch" rule is respected. This charges the situation even more with sensual tension.

The tease never stops

The fact that you are not with your partner does not mean that the "tease and denial" stops. A phone is enough to drive your partner crazy and make sure that sexual tension builds throughout the day.

Send your partner some nudes while you are both at work, leave a sexy voice message or try some phone sex during lunch break.

If the fear of being caught red-handed excites you, why not try to assign some tasks to your partner to be carried out in a public place?

I like to send my man some nudes and ask him to find a private place at work to masturbate. Of course, he can not cum, but he must go as close to orgasm as possible. This is called edging, and trust me, when he gets home in the evening, he only has one thing on his mind.

Do you really need panties?

Try to do housework without panties or if you feel more adventurous, go for a walk in a public place and forget your panties at home. Then, flash him "accidentally" when he least expects it. You could also go further and ask your partner to give you oral pleasure but without reciprocating.

I remember one year when we went camping, my man's tongue has never been so busy in his entire life.

Masturbate in front of your partner

A much more straightforward way to turn your partner on is to masturbate in front of him. He will be faced with what he craves most, but you can deny him from reaching it.

Start a quick makeout or oral sex session

If you want to go further, then start a quickie; the important thing is to stop before the point of no return. The same criteria can be applied to oral sex. You can slowly excite your partner, just enough to get his engine running, and then stop before he takes off.

6.3 Bondage

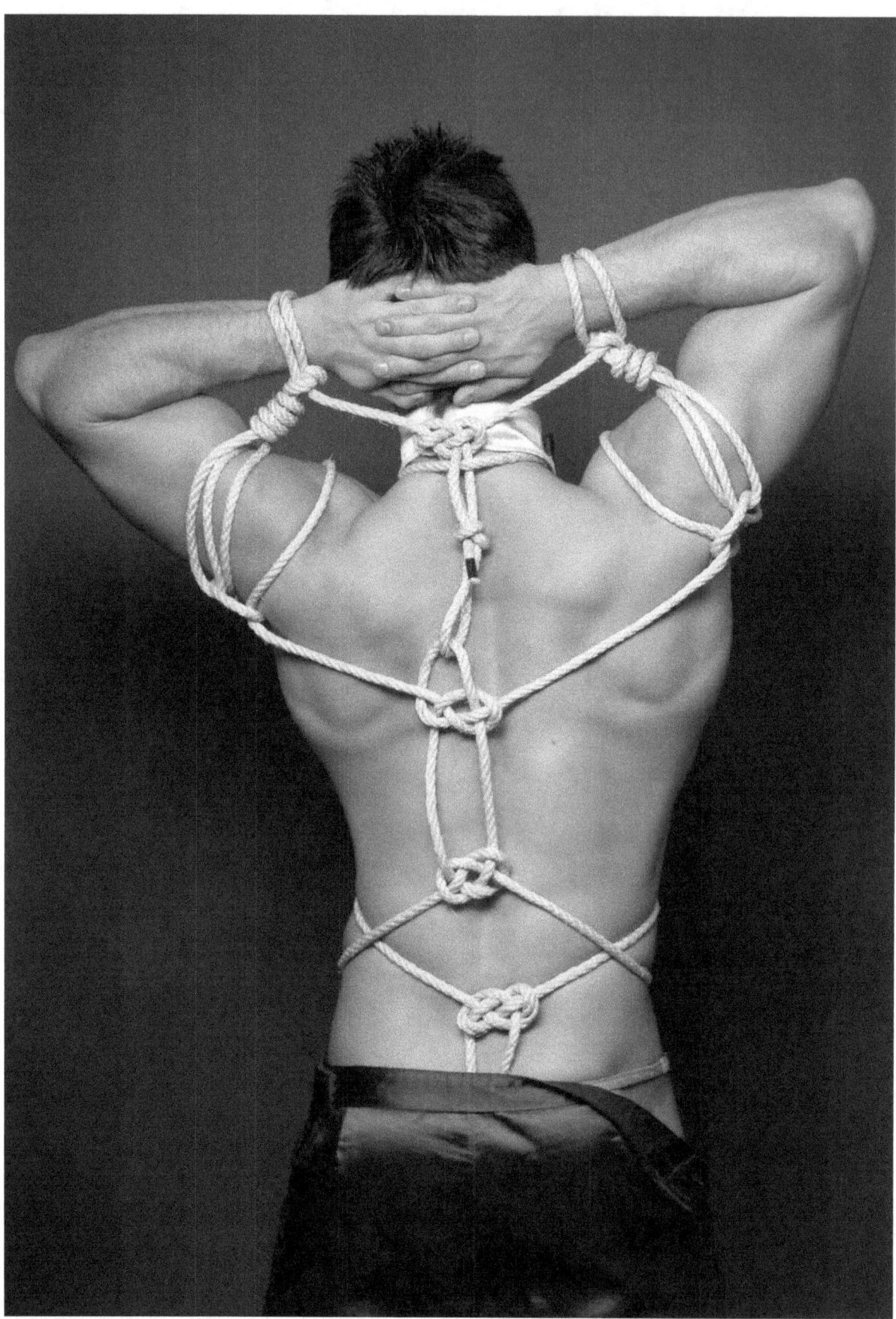

Bondage is a common fantasy, and it represents the B in BDSM (Bondage, Discipline, Sadism, and Masochism). Wikipedia has a great definition of bondage: "…is the practice of consensually tying, binding, or restraining a partner for erotic, aesthetic, or somatosensory stimulation. It means the need to tie someone up or be tied up. A partner may be physically restrained in a variety of ways, including the use of rope, cuffs, bondage tape, or self-adhering bandage." So many people incorporate different levels of bondage into their sex lives; think about how many models of fluffy handcuffs there are around. Going deep into the topic would require a book of its own. What I would try to do in this section is giving you some basic principles and ideas that you can try with your partner. If both of you are interested in this practice, I would suggest you buy a book dedicated solely to the subject and/or watch the various video tutorials available online.

Whether you are an expert or a novice, it is essential to approach this technique as safely as possible. These are basic safety guidelines that you should always follow:

- <u>Use a safeword</u> or some clear way for the bound partner to stop the game.
- <u>Never leaving a bound person alone.</u>
- To avoid circulation problems, make sure that the bound person changes positions at least once an hour.
- Make sure that you can quickly release the bound person in case of an emergency.
- <u>Avoid restraints that impair breathing.</u>
- Have scissors on hand in case of a problem that requires cutting a rope.

Here a few beginners' ideas you could try:

Beginner's Luck

With this, you can avoid using ropes and feel bound. It is perfect if you want to give it a try but not fully commit. One of the partners lies on the bed with the hands behind their back. The other person can have fun, having their disposal of the fully exposed partner's body.

The Full Spread

You will need a spreader bar or just some bondage tape and a broom handle for this position.

The receiver is in all fours with the bar attached to the ankles. This forces the receiver's ankles apart and gives easy access to their butt. In this position, the giver can be creative and use toys, mouth, hands, or penetration to stimulate the receiver.

The Naughty Chair

For this position, you will require three pieces of rope that will be used to secure the receiver to *"The Naughty Chair."* First, the receiver sits backward on a hard, armless chair. The receiver then stands leaning on the back of the chair while their butt hangs over the front edge. Next, the first two pieces of ropes are used to bind the receiver ankles to the front chair legs. Next, to complete the opera, the receiver's hands are tied behind the back with the third. This position is perfect for some roleplay situations and anal sex. It also allows for a quick release and causes only slight discomfort.

The X Factor

This position requires four pieces of rope or, if you want to go pro, you can buy are under the bed restraint system. The receiver lies on the bed in a face-down position. Arms and legs are tied to the corners of the bed so that the receiver's body forms an X. This position is perfect for beginners since it is incredibly comfortable and being face down feels less exposing.

Pass the Velvet Rope

This position can be achieved both in a standing and lying position. For a standing position, you can use restraints that fit over a door. Depending on your preferences, you could position the receiver's back against the door or towards you. If you decide to adopt the standing position, then the receiver's wrists are secured over the head to the door. If you choose to use the lying position, then the wrists are tied to the bed's headboard. In both cases, the genitals or butt, depending on which direction the receiver is facing, are exposed. You could try to use only your mouth to touch the receiver's body, or you might have different ideas!

On the Ropes

In this position, the receiver kneels with their face on the bed. The left Ankle is tied to the left wrist, and the right ankle is linked to the right wrist in a position that resembles doggy style. This position is perfect for anal play since the receiver's bum is completely exposed, but it can be used, also, for amazing handjobs.

In a variation of this position, the receiver is lying on the back and is bound precisely in the same way. In this way, the genitals of the receiver are entirely exposed to the giver's attention.

6.4 Foot fetish

Academic studies have found that feet and foot accessories are the most fetishized of all non-genital body parts and objects. Nearly half of all such fetishes focus on feet, and almost two-thirds of fetishes for objects associated with the body are for shoes and socks. The most probable reason for that has been found in the fact that the areas of the brain related to genitals and feet are adjacent. Therefore, a lot of people have their brains wired in a way that they find feet sexy! If you or your partner are among them, it is worth discussing the topic and exploring the idea. Of course, there is nothing wrong with being attracted from parts of the body other than the genitals, buttocks, or breasts. However, taboos are finally starting to break down in today's society, and a person should not be ashamed to discuss his sexual urges with the person he loves. Feet are sexy and can be incorporated into your games. Try to wear a nice pair of heels and nice stockings, and use your extremities to massage your partner's body, including the genitals.

Besides, kissing the feet and licking the toes is a common practice that can be included in the foreplay.

6.5 Spanking

Spanking is an ancient practice; earlier depictions of erotic spanking can be found in the Etruscan Tomb of the Whipping from the fifth century BC.

This practice was present in the original Kama Sutra (400 BC), which suggested its use to enhance sexual arousal. The 20th century is considered the *"golden age"* of spanking literature, with the distributions of many spanking novels accompanied by illustrations. However, this golden age came to an end due to the introduction, in Europe, of various censorship laws during the second world war. Recently, the proliferation of the internet has allowed many individuals to get in touch with each other and start spreading material on the subject again.

Spanking can be administered with the bare hand, but also tools can be used. The variety of spanking tools is immense, among the most famous we can find:

- Cane
- Paddle
- Slipper
- Wooden spoon
- Carpet beater

Depending on the tool used, the sensation transmitted will be different. For instance, a cane gives a *"stingy"* feeling, a sharp and quick-burning sense mostly felt on the skin. On the other hand, being spanked with a paddle gives a *"thuddy"* sensation that penetrates deeper into the body tissues.

Safety is always essential in these types of practices; mainly when you are using spanking tools, it is crucial to avoid striking the tailbone and the hipbones of the receiver.

Spanking is excellent combined with roleplay; for instance, you could try a teacher-student scenario and punish your naughty partner with a ruler.

Soft spanking, with the bare hand, can be used during the foreplay or in the most aroused phases of sexual intercourse. Although, I have to admit that I don't mind a good spanking while I'm in doggy style!

6.6 Anal play & sex

A few years ago, it was much more challenging to talk about anal play and anal sex, while nowadays, you cannot see a comedy show without hearing at least three jokes about anal sex, pegging, and its derivatives. Despite this, the general impression is that there is still a bit of shame to talk about it openly. Well, let me tell you, anal sex is incredible! You do not have to have an anal fetish to take part in anal sex; however, many individuals explicitly get off on butt stuff. Anal play can go from adding a finger in the ass during penetrative vaginal sex to utilizing butt attachments to having anal sex with a penis or a dildo. In a new report, 37 percent of ladies and 43 percent of men said they had tried anal sex (in which ladies got and men gave). "The anal opening and canal have a wealth of nerve endings that are primed for pleasure," says Caitlin V., MPH, clinical sexologist for Royal. This means that anyone can experience pleasure, sometimes even orgasm, from anal stimulation, regardless of gender or genitals. If you are interested in the topic, I will give you some ideas about the most common practices in this section.

Clean yourself

Before starting anal sex, whether you are a man or a woman, it is recommended to clean up the area to avoid unpleasant inconveniences. A shower or a wet wipe can do the job. In addition, it is advisable to empty the bowels 45 minutes before intercourse.

Use a lot of lube

The critical thing to keep always in your mind is that the anus does not self-lubricate. Therefore, to avoid painful problems, it is advisable to use a good quantity of lubricant. The choice of the type of lubricant depends on what objects you are going to use for penetration.

- Use a **silicone-based lube** if you are playing with fingers or objects made in wood or stainless steel.
- Use a **water-based lube** if you are using a silicone toy.

Get relaxed and in the mood

It is essential to be relaxed before starting any anal play or anal sex activity. The anus is an extremely sensitive area, and in the act of penetration, if the recipient has contracted muscles, there is a risk of causing micro-injuries. Natural ways for relaxing are a warm bath, essential oils, deep breathing, or just playing with yourself. In addition, stimulating your genitals or other erogenous zones and becoming aroused will significantly relax your muscles in the area.

Also, remember to start slowly and gently; you have to give your body time to get used to it.

Anal activities

There are different activities that you could, alone or with your partner.
Anal sex: Well, this is self-explanatory. I suggest starting with doggy style or with the receiver lying on the back. These are the most accessible position and allow for the maximum spread of the area.
Prostate stimulation: Guess what, men G-Spot is the prostate, and it can

be reached through anal stimulation. There are specific toys designed to stimulate the prostate on the market, but it can be done with your fingers as well. The important thing is to use a good amount of lube and take it at your own pace. Finding the prostate is not complex; you could do this massage yourself or with the help of your partner.:

- Apply lube.
- Insert the index finger slowly to the first knuckle, to it a couple of times applying lube.
- When you feel the area is well-lubricated, insert up to the second knuckle and repeat the previous steps until you reach the third knuckle.
- Once the finger is comfortably inserted, search for a rounded lump roughly 4 inches inside the rectum and up towards the root of the penis. This is the prostate, and it is extremely sensitive.
- You can massage the prostate in a circular motion or back and forth but gently.

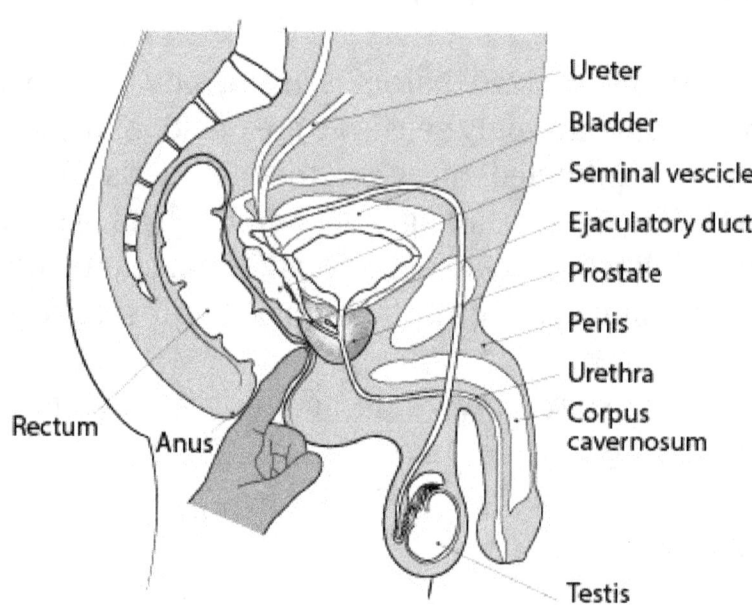

Pegging: This practice is fantastic and gives the woman an incredible sense of power. It consists of penetrating her man with a strap-on dildo. For pegging, a double ending dildo can be used; one side can penetrate the anus while the other is inserted in the vagina. I have tried this practice with my man a few times, and we both loved it. What I can suggest is to start small and with a double-ended dildo. There are strap-ons on the market that do not require any harnesses, but I have personally found hard to use them. I do prefer the harness version, which is much more stable. Also, consider buying one with a vibration function for extra pleasure.

Butt plugs: They can be an excellent addition to your sex life; butt plugs are specifically designed to be inserted into the rectum, even for long periods. These toys are generally smooth and short and can be used during sex by both men and women to provide additional stimulation to the rectum. So if you want to try some light butt stuff and have a different stimulation during sex, butt plugs are what you are looking for.

6.7 Beyond the bedroom

In The Bathroom

From the edge of the sink to the side of the shower, the washroom is brimming with perfect spots to push back on when you and your accomplice next get the desire to have sex. Likewise, the shower is ideal for a sensual encounter – all that running water, shower oil, and a lot of snares and edges to grasp – incredible for those couples who appreciate sex in a standing position.

In The Kitchen

The kitchen tabletop is a classic used in numerous movies on the big screen, yet why not try it for yourself at home. There are plenty of positions that adapt perfectly to kitchen surfaces, and this room is accompanied by many interesting objects. For example, you could play with some ice cubes on your partner's body, administer some nice spanking with a spatula or tie your accomplice to the fridge handles while having sex in a standing position. Every room can be your pleasure room if you use a little creativity.

In The Car

Whenever you and your accomplice are on an excursion, return yourself to those insidious teen years, and stop the vehicle on a peaceful dirt road with no traffic. Then, push back the front seats and jump on top of your accomplice in the driving seat for some sex on the road or move both over the backseats where there will be more space to try various positions.

The Woods

If you both share a love for nature, and you have fun camping in the woods, then why not try here? If you can find a sufficiently isolated place, then you could make a portion of the forest your bedroom. Trees are great to lean against, and they can give you the support to try the most varied positions. Also, you will not have to contain your moans of pleasure if there is no one around.

In the Rain

Have you tried having sex in the shower and enjoyed it? Then, why not trying having sex under a summer shower? Whether you like it or not, you will have another memorable experience, and in my case, a cold, having tried it in October.

Under the Stars

Find a place with a good view; it could be a top of a hill, a rooftop, or the bed of a truck. Whatever allows you to see the sky without the light pollution of the city. A starry sky above your head and the person you love next to you is the perfect recipe to create an unforgettable moment. Bring a couple of glasses and some chilled wine with you; this is the ideal scenario for making love and abandoning yourself entirely in your partner's arms.

6.8 Cuckolding

Ok, this is not for everyone. However, suppose you are not familiar with Cuckolding. In that case, I think the definition provided by Chris Riotta could help: "the term alludes to when a man or woman has sex with a partner who is already married to someone else. Sometimes, it is out of wedlock, and the experience is essentially just cheating with a fancy term. Other times, it's a fetish in which some married partners enjoy watching their spouse have sex with other partners."

As I said, this is not for everyone, I think I would go crazy to see my man having sex with another woman, but plenty of people find this idea intriguing. Cuckolding can be experienced at different levels, and it is not always necessary to have relationships with another person. Very often, the very idea of betrayal creates a sense of humiliation in the cuckold that is enough to turn him on.

Here some ideas that you might want to try if you are into this.

Go Shopping for your Lover

Bring your partner with you while shopping for your lover; even worse, make your partner pay for everything you will buy. For example, lingerie shopping is perfect. You could try on different underwear and make it clear that you are buying it to arouse someone else. Verbal play in this type of situation is essential; saying things like "I think X will love fucking me in this black underwear" would turn on any cuckold on the face of the earth.

Flirt Openly with Strangers

While your partner is watching, start to flirt with people in bars or lounges. Have your partner find a seat across the room, where they have a nice view of the situation. If the conversation gets a little bit intimate, then you can decide what to do; you might want to go all the way or stop after a few touches and whispers.

Your Cock is Not Big Enough

In this scenario, you want to humiliate your partner, mentioning the size of your (hypothetical?) lovers; for most women, size matters to a degree. Humiliation is a big part of being a cuckold, and being compared to partner lovers is a source of excitement for many of them.

Use Chastity Devices

A common practice during cuckold play is to force the partner to use a chastity device. The basic idea is that you own and manage his orgasms as you please. Who owns the rights to the partner's orgasms is commonly called keyholder since, in most cases, they hold the key to unlock the chastity device. There are chastity devices for both genders on the market, which can also be worn for long periods. However, chastity belts allow you to perform incredibly long and frustrating tease and denial sessions, which can be pushed to the extreme preventing the partner from having an orgasm even for long periods.

Cuckolding and chastity are two vast and complex worlds that would need a book of their own. In this section, I have limited myself to mentioning their existence and providing some basic ideas. If you think these activities are of your interest, I advise you to look for specific texts on the subject; I do not believe I would do justice to these topics in these few lines.

6.9 Food play

Food can easily be incorporated into your bedroom activities. In addition, many playful ideas can be easily implemented to make sex a lot more interesting.

Cherries

Why not start with a classic? For example, you could challenge your partner to the classic kissing test to see who can tie a cherry stem in a knot with their tongue. Also, cherries are great (especially if cold) to run over your partner's body sensually. Their juice can be drizzled over their erogenous zones and tasted with some tongue play.

Popsicles

Yes, they resemble penises and can be used to show off your blowjob skills. In addition, they are perfect for some foreplay or tease and denial. You could quickly drive your partner crazy at the thought that his penis might be in your mouth instead of the popsicle.

Grapes

Grapes are the perfect fruit if you want to do some roleplay and become queen for one night. Let your partner feed you, one grape at a time, "Cleopatra style." Also, frozen grapes can be used for temperature play. Have your love pluck a frozen grape from its stem and run it over your nipple and other erogenous zones.

Whipped Cream

Yes, I know, it is a little obvious, but I love whipped cream! Spread it on some erogenous zones of your choice and serve an unforgettable dessert to your partner! Penis shafts are fun to decorate with whipped cream, but I suggest not inserting the dessert inside the labia since sugar can cause yeast infections.

Chocolate syrup

If you like whipped cream, then this is the next level. It is a little messier and requires more tongue work to lick it off your lover, but it is also a lot of fun. Also, if you feel creative, you could use it to draw or write messages on your partner's body.

6.10 Sensory deprivation

The idea behind sensory deprivation is to limit one or more senses during sex to sharpen the rest. The basic idea is to experience sexual intercourse on another level by amplifying sensations that would not have the same impact in the presence of all the senses.

Sight deprivation

Something as simple as wearing a blindfold or switching off the lights can be remarkably exciting. If you do not see what is about to happen, fear and curiosity will act as amplifiers of the sensations you are experiencing.

Sound-play

Blocking out sounds using wireless headphones can be a powerful weapon. Instead of using white noise, I prefer to pick some music that can better contextualize the moment. For example, if you feel particularly kinky, why not play an audio of people moaning with pleasure.

VR experience

If you have a VR headset, you should try this technique. Have your partner sit in a chair with the headset on and headphones with noise cancellation. Pick porn that your partner likes and show it to them in VR if you have a second screen, even better since you will be able to see what your partner is seeing. Your partner will be almost totally isolated from the outside world, and your goal will be to make the VR experience even more immersive. Stimulate them as you see fit; you can touch his erogenous zones, give them oral sex, or simply let them feel the heat of your body by rubbing on them. The experience will be even more incredible if you contextualize the stimulations with what they see on the screen.

6.11 Sex toys

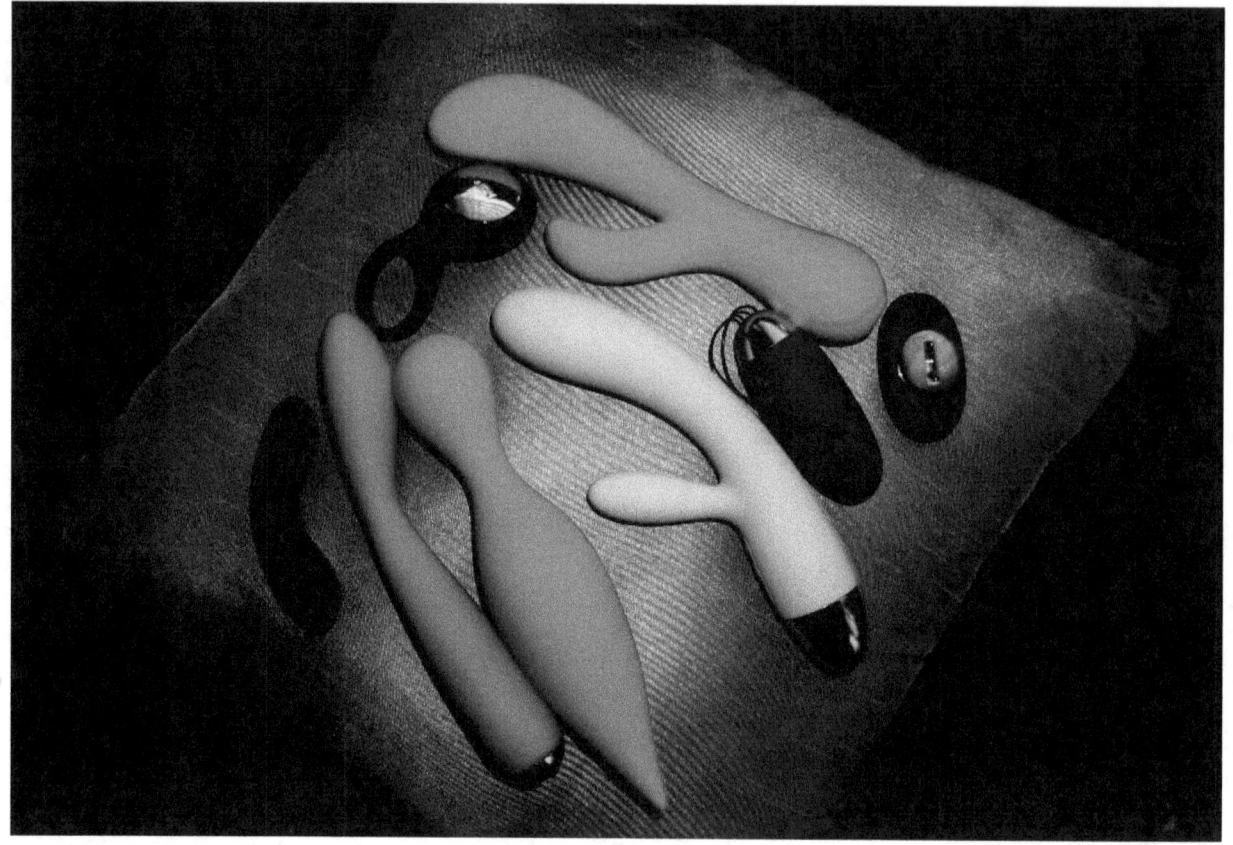

By now on the market, there are dozens of sex toys for the most diverse tastes. Here is a list of the most famous and their functions. I am sure you will find some that will pique your interest.

Dildos

Such things are made in different sizes, shapes, and shadings. It ought to be noticed that the male penis, on average 15-18 cm, when dildos, can arrive at 35-40 cm long. Dildos are incredibly versatile and can be an excellent prelude to sex. They can help to get excited and warm up your body before sex.

The most common types are:

- **Silicone dildos:** Unlike those in rubber, they cannot cause allergic reactions. They are smooth and firm, perfect for vaginal and rectal activities.
- **Vibrating dildos:** They use a series of sophisticated micromotors to introduce different levels of vibration. They usually cost more, but the incredible additional stimulation justifies the cost.
- **Inflatable dildos:** These dildos are designed to inflate once inserted! They are typically made of flexible latex or rubber, and some can incorporate vibrations functions as well. For example, you can pump up them with air creating a full-up feeling that stretches you to satisfaction.
- **Glass dildos:** They are made of borosilicate glass; the firm material is perfect for G-Spot or prostate stimulation.
- **Double-ended dildos:** They are great for sharing with your partner. They come in an incredible range of sizes, and they are made of bendable and twistable materials. You will be able to try positions that you did not suspect existed before.
- **Anal dildos:** Their shape is specifically designed for anal play. They are often slimmer and designed to stimulate the rectum and the prostate.

Vaginal balls

Kegel balls or *Ben Wa balls* have been used for centuries to increase the strength of pelvic and vagile floor muscles. However, nowadays, they are mainly used for enhancing sexual pleasure; for this reason, they are also called *Venus balls* or orgasms balls.

Vaginal balls are not used in the same way as traditional sex toys; to get the maximum pleasure, you must leave them inside, and they will multiply your fun during masturbation.

Magic wand

This was initially marketed as a general body massager for sore muscles until the '70s when it became famous for its secondary use, one of the best vibrators for clitoral stimulation.

Butt plugs

These are designed to be inserted into the rectum and come in different sizes and sets. Unlike dildos, they are intended to be left inserted even for relatively long periods and can be worn to amplify the sensations resulting from regular sexual activity.

Rabbit vibrators

This is the sex toy no girl should be without! These vibrators are great for clitoral stimulators, and the shaft guarantees intense and extended orgasms. It is also suitable for anal stimulation in case you want to try something different.

6.12 Aphrodisiacs

An aphrodisiac is a food or a substance that, when ingested, drives individuals to turn out to be sexually stimulated. Numerous individuals will utilize these as a fun and coy approach to get them and add their accomplice in the temperament for sex.

Liquor, Marijuana, and Drugs

Cannabis and liquor are the two aphrodisiacs that work by bringing down restraints in the psyche. Suppose you have at any point been affected by both of these. In that case, you may have seen that you felt more secure when it came to stroll over to the bar to converse with that appealing individual you had been looking at or that you were more forward in your sexual advances with your accomplice. This is because these substances brought down your hindrances, which permitted your sexual driving forces to take the driver's seat and persuaded you to do things that you, in any case, would not have because of the expanded sensations of excitement that you were encountering.

Ginseng

Ginseng is a spice that is frequently utilized in Chinese Medicine. In addition, it is extensively used to treat erectile dysfunctions and can prompt more noteworthy degrees of sexual excitement in ladies. It can be ingested in different ways, yet the most well-known route in Asia is ginseng tea.

Pistachio

Pistachio nuts are demonstrated to be an aphrodisiac. These nuts are found in various dishes, both flavorful and sweet, and can be ingested entirety. Pistachios are used, in some cultures, to cure erectile dysfunction in men as it increases bloodstream. In ladies, it can cause increased sexual excitement. Other than being aphrodisiacs, pistachios have numerous other medical advantages, including weight control and improving heart functionalities.

Saffron

This rare and expensive spice must be collected by hand, and many flowers are required to make just a few grams. Historically, it has been utilized as a solution for tiredness and psychological issues. Nowadays, it has been theorized that this spice can help increase sexual appetite.

Saffron is a powerful aphrodisiac, and it is used with individuals who are on antidepressants since it can help balance the diminished sexual drive they cause.

Chocolate

The Aztecs may have been the first on record to draw a link between the cocoa bean and sexual drive. Nowadays, we know that the aphrodisiac qualities of chocolate are due to two substances contains tryptophan and phenylethylamine. So, consuming chocolate can help increase sexual appetite and provide the right amount of energy for a memorable night.

Oysters

It is a widespread belief that oysters are a powerful aphrodisiac.
There is no scientific basis to support this theory, but indeed an excellent fish-based dinner can put anyone in the best mood. It is probably not a great idea to play in bed with oysters but organizing a romantic candlelit oyster-based dinner will help to spark the passion.

Honey

Honey has been considered an aphrodisiac for centuries; the very word honeymoon stems from the hope for a sweet marriage. It is known that Hippocrates prescribed honey for sexual vigor, and in an old French tale, receiving a bee sting was like being given a shot of pure aphrodisiac. For these reasons, honey is the symbol of fertility and procreation in many cultures. At the chemical level, honey contains a substance called boron that can contribute to regulating hormone levels. Playing with honey in bed can be messy but sweet (literally).

6.13 Exercises to improve sexual performance

Some may not like hearing it, but an excellent physical condition generally leads to improved quality of sexual intercourse. Without going to extremes, with the stories of people who have had a heart attack while having sex, improving your physical condition can increase the duration and intensity of the performance. Doing physical activity activates specific processes in the body that are similar to those activated during sexual intercourse. We all know that having sex increases sweating, heart activity, and blood flow, just as it would with a running session.

Having sex can be considered physical activity; some studies have calculated that, for each minute, 4.2 calories are burned on average for men and 3.1 for women; the problem is the average duration of sex, which is around 20 minutes. This implies that the total calories burned are not high. For these reasons, it is best to try to burn our calories and get in shape by going to the gym or doing other sports activities.

To increase sexual performance, which muscle groups should we focus on, and what type of training? Of course, the answer is pelvic floor muscles!

The following tips focus on making the most significant possible impact on your performance in bed without having to turn into a pro athlete.

20 Minutes training

The following routine does not require any gym equipment, and it should take only 20minutes. I started doing it twice a week, and after a month, I have already begun to see the first results!

Set a timer to 20 minutes and repeat the following exercises until the timer goes off.
- **Planks:** Plant your forearms on the floor with elbows below your shoulders. Ground toes into the floor and squeeze glutes to stabilize your body. Put your head in line with your back. Hold the position for 30 seconds.
- **Glute bridge:** Start flat on your back with legs bent at a 90-degree angle and feet placed flat on the ground. Turn your toes at a 45-degree angle and align your knees to face in the same direction. Push your hips up, keeping the knees over your toes throughout the entire movement. Let your hips sink back and repeat (this counts as one repetition). Perform three sets of 15 repetitions.
- **Jump squat:** Stand with your feet shoulder-width apart. Start by doing a regular squat, then engage your core and jump up. When you land, lower your body back into a squat position to complete one repetition. Do two sets of 10 repetitions.
- **Kegels:** Ensure that your bladder is empty, then sit down. Tighten your pelvic floor muscles. Hold tight and count 3 to 5 seconds. Next, relax the muscles and count 3 to 5 seconds. Perform two sets of 10 repetitions.
- **Pushups:** Start in a high plank position with your palms flat. Bend your elbows and lower your chest to the floor. Push through the palms of your hands to straighten your arms. This counts as one reap. Perform three sets of 8 repetitions.

Try Yoga

Yoga is the discipline par excellence to improve your sexual performance; not only can it be used as stress relief, but it increases the flexibility of the body, coordination and strengthens the core muscles Yoga. Suppose you are a particularly emotional or stressed person. In that case, you will find immense benefits in practicing yoga since it reduces cortisol levels, one of the leading causes of stress.

"Yoga teaches you how to listen to your body and how to control your mind," says Lauren Zoeller, a certified yoga instructor and Whole Living Life Coach based in Nashville, Tennessee. "These two practices combined can bring your insight on what you like and dislike, leading you to communicate better what is best to your partner."

If you want to try Yoga, I suggest looking for a course close to home so you can learn the basics from a professional. I will list here the yoga positions that, in my experience, have the most significant impact in terms of stress relief and fitness improvement. I would suggest that you perform them supervised by a professional so that you can learn the correct execution of each position.

Cat Pose – Marjaryasana / Cow Pose – Bitilasana

    This is a gentle flow between two positions that mainly involves the back muscles and the spine. The starting position is on hands and knees with knees under the hips and hands under the shoulders, head in a neutral position. To move into Bitilasana, inhale and drop your belly towards the mat. Gaze up towards the sky, lifting chin and chest. Open your shoulders and relax, feeling the stretch on the spine. To transition into Marjaryasana, exhale and draw your belly to your spine while rounding the back towards the sky. Release your head towards the floor. Repeat the cycle up to 20 times.

Bridge Pose – Setu Bandha Sarvangasana

Lie on your back with knees bent and feet firmly on the floor. Place your arms on either side of your body with your palms facing down. Exhale as you lift your hips towards the sky while pressing both feet and arms into the floor. Roll your shoulders back. The only parts in contact with the floor must be your arms, feet, head, and upper back.

Happy Baby – Ananda Balasana

Lie on your back, and while exhaling, bend your knees into your belly. Inhale and grip your feet or toes with your hands. Open your knees slightly wider than your torso and bring them up toward your armpits. Be sure that each ankle is positioned over the knee.

Child's Pose – Balasana

Come to your hands and knees on the mat. Slightly spread your knees and keep the top of your feet on the floor. Bend, bringing your forehead to the floor. It is essential to relax your spine, shoulders, and jaw. Stay as long as you like, feeling the nice stretch on your spine.

Corpse Pose – Savasana

Lie on your back with legs and arms straight, palms facing upward. Stay as long as you like focusing on your breathing.

While some yoga poses can immediately improve your sex life, the most significant change will always reduce your stress. Not only does this provide a whole host of benefits, but it also allows you to relax and enjoy sex, which makes it even better.

The Invisible Chair Exercise

This exercise is perfect for those with little time and no equipment. To perform "the invisible chair," put your back flat against a wall with your hands open on the surface of the wall. Next, bring your legs forward and flex your knees until you reach a position where you are sitting supported only by the wall. Once this is done, try to hold the position as long as possible. Repeat for at least three times with 60 seconds of rest between each attempt. This exercise is a simple, easy and effective way to work your core and lower body, so grab a wall and relax in your "Invisible Chair"!

Conclusion

I wrote this book with the idea of sharing what I have learned from my experiences around the world and my passion for Indian culture.
I hope, in this manuscript, you found what you were looking for, be it a new position, some new ideas, or topics to start a conversation with your partner to deepen your relationship.

As you have learned by now, the Kama Sutra is not just a series of sexual positions; it is a way of approaching a relationship, love, and life in general. Moreover, the original text consisted of more than 500 pages, some difficult to interpret, others totally out of context for modern times. For these reasons, I have not tried to provide my readers with an exact copy of the original work. I tried instead to extract the parts that, in my opinion, are most relevant in modern society, and I have mixed them with some suggestions and ideas from my personal experience. I hope the result was exciting and that I was able to convey the fundamental principles of the Kama Sutra to you.

If there is one thing that I mainly wanted to convey to you, it is the idea that there is no right or wrong in making love.

Two or more people are free to experience everything they want to try together and thus seek new incredible sensations.

It is essential to cultivate love and try new experiences, especially in relationships that we believe have been solid and have lasted for many years. This allows us to continue to renew the flame of passion and live a whole and happy life.

www.ingramcontent.com/pod-product-compliance
Lightning Source LLC
LaVergne TN
LVHW062244070526
838201LV00093B/175

9 7 9 1 2 8 0 7 6 2 2 7 6